ONE HELICOPTER PILOT'S EXPERIENCES

CAPT. E. RAY POSS JR.

Hardcover: 978-1-964035-52-9
Paperback: 978-1-964035-50-5
eBook: 978-1-964035-51-2
Library of Congress Control Number: 2024922348

This is a work of nonfiction.

SWEETSPIRE LITERATURE
—— MANAGEMENT ——

Table of Contents

Dedications

As far back as I can remember, so many have told me to write a book. Please remember that, I'm a helicopter pilot's when reading.

There is so many stories that I could write about and maybe I'll write more stories in the future.

For those of you that wanted the stories I have told over the years. Thank you for wanting these stories and having me write them.

I hope you enjoy.

Ray

My Childhood

D ad was a very hard worker always doing something and doing it very well. I can remember watching Dad build a project with no plans or supply list. When he would start a project, he always had the blueprint in his head. I was always amazed when he finished the job, there were no scraps. It didn't matter if it was concrete work, brick, carpentry or metal, dad knew how to do it all. I'm sure Dad acquired his skills when he worked for the C.C.C. camp. I know that during WWII Dad was classified as 4 F because he was flat footed and started working in the shipyard in Houston Texas as a welder. During the depression the President started the C.C.C. camp for construction projects to keep men employed. One project that I know Dad worked on was the path leading through the Carlsbad Caverns in New Mexico. The 1.25 mile (2 km) Natural Entrance Trail is extremely steep. Depending on if you decide to hike up or down, you gain or lose about 750 feet (229 m)—equivalent to walking up or down a 75-story building. The hike takes about one hour (on average) to complete.

Stairway down into Carlsbad Caverns New Mexico

He was very kind and gentle always looking out for you. As the oldest I've felt privileged to work with dad and go with him on Saturdays to his work at Cormier Chevrolet. Dad was respected by all and a pleasure to be around. I remember my first car, a gentleman brought in a 1951 Chevrolet to the garage were dad worked and needed work on the engine. After checking out the engine the price for repair was more than the car was worth. Dad offered the man $50.00 for the car and purchased it. He then overhauled the engine, had the Body Shop cherry the body and paint it, and the upholstery shop do a custom interior. When he was finished the car was in excellent shape and I drove it with pride. One night I was coming home way past my curfew after a date with my girlfriend, so I turned off the engine just before I came to the house and turned into the driveway thinking I was so smart. However, the brakes did not work, and I crashed thru the garage door and into Mom's Pink Cadillac. Of course, it woke Dad up and out he came. He couldn't believe what I had done and just started to repair the damage at 2am. On closer inspection there was no damage to Mom's Cadillac (Thank God) Dad said nothing to me at the time.

Don and I shared a room with bunk beds, and I decided to cover the ceiling with bamboo poles and Palm Frans. I had placed lighting above them and for sure it was a cool room. However, one night the bamboo poles had shrunk, and the ceiling came down on us. Not so cool, but Don never complained.

In 1960 my senior year at Millikan High School in Long Beach CA, dad helped me purchase a 1959 Chevrolet Impala. I can remember dad telling me boy whatever you do don't lower the car. Of course, as a teen age know it all, I slowly lowered the car until it was on the bottom. I joined a car club in High School called the Rum Runners.

The club was a lot of fun and a great group of guys. We would sponsor poker runs throughout the Las Angeles County. On one of the poker runs I had a broken foot with a walker cast. I was working one of the check points, and it started raining. When the run was completed, I had no cast on my foot. The next morning mom took me to the doctor, and he wanted to know what happened. When I told him, he laughed and said well your very lucky there was no damage.

I had a 1959 triumph motorcycle and a friend of mine had just purchased a brand-new bike. We decided to go for a 200-mile ride Saturday morning to break it in. After the 200 miles, he stated he was ready to race me. I told him he could maybe pass me once we reached 100. I was right when we reach that speed he started pulling ahead. We were coming close to where we needed to turn, and he didn't know the way. I riffed my engine and when he heard it, he hit his brakes and my front wheel went between his rear wheel and left exhaust stack. It forced my bike down and I was riding on top doing almost 100 mph. I could see a 1959 Oldsmobile with all four tires smoking coming straight for me. I have no idea what I did, but I managed to get the bike back up on two wheels. I missed the Oldsmobile and flew into a lake. After cleaning the plugs with carbon tet, I drove home. Dad was watering the front lawn when I arrived, and he asked if that was me making all that noise a few minutes ago. I pretended I didn't know what he was talking about. I cleaned up the bike, put a for sale sign on it, and that ended by motorcycle career.

When I graduated, I went straight into the Navy and sold the Impala. When preparing the car for sale dad put new Springs in the car and raised it back to the factory height. The gentleman that bought the car stated he would never own a car that had been lowered by a teenager. (LOL)

After I was discharged from the Navy I went to work with dad and learned his trade as an auto mechanic but, I had always wanted to be a pilot so one day I gave him my roll-a-way of tools and quit to take flying lessons. Dad was appalled that I thought I could be a pilot and thought I was crazy. After completing pilot training and obtaining my pilot license, he thought if I could do it so could he. So, dad got his private airplane license. Dad became ill with Parkinson's disease, and close to the end dad called the four boys altogether and stated that he wanted us to promise to have him cremated and Scatter his ashes at sunrise or sunset over Red Rock Canyon outside of Las Vegas. I promised him that his wish would be carried out. When dad passed, mom wanted us to bury him, but I told her I had promised dad he would be cremated. Mom stated she didn't care and did not want her husband cremated. I told mom fine, we would bury him, but when she passed, we would dig him up and cremate both of them. Mom was adamantly against being cremated and stated, well darling how much will it cost to cremate him. Well I guess there is always more than one way to skin a cat!

Dad would always tease the children by asking them if they wanted ice cream. When they said yes, he would then hold out his fist and say here you go; do you want chocolate, strawberry, or vanilla. I think of dad often and really miss him.

Mom was an incredible lady, and always dressed to the nines. She was the glue that held the

Dad

family together. As a child growing up, I remember for breakfast she always made biscuits and gravy, bacon, sausage, eggs, pancakes and oatmeal. I guess with four boys she wanted to make sure we all ate and were satisfied. Mom was always there for us and very understanding even with 4 boys. In 1957, mom told dad day she wanted a pink Cadillac, so of course dad bought her a new 1957 Pink Cadillac

One day Mom came home with a half dozen ping pong paddles with attached rubber band to the red rubber balls. We thought that was great until she snapped off the rubber bands … we knew it wasn't good. She told us she was tired of us growing boys laughing when she swatted us for the latest transgressions and was going to place the paddles around the house to be close when needed. Mom was about 5 ft tall and us boys were taller and growing but she always ruled the roost with us. We knew for certain we were in trouble when she said, 'just wait till your dad gets home!'. Dad would always show up in a good mood and glad to be home from work, until mom said, "Honey do you know what your son did?" You could see dad's face as she made her statement, he really didn't want to deal with it. The look was always followed by, "Boy, this is going to hurt me more than it hurts you." Maybe you have also heard this statement.

With no Air conditioner back then, when it was hot, mom would shew us boys out 'to play' and tell us to be back when the streetlight came on.

I can remember one of the many times that I was introduced to the paddle. Don had been bothering me while I was trying to watch TV. He was talking loudly and laughing so I took one of his dirty socks and stuffed it in his mouth. That shut him up for a while until mom and dad came home, then the usual happened when he screamed, "Mom Ray put a dirty sock in my mouth" I think you get the picture.

When Don came home on leave from the Airforce, dad had drained the pool and had us painting it. Don and I were in the pool with Larry and Jerry quietly following our movements above, dripping drops of paint on us. Shirtless, we didn't feel it because Larry was trying to see how much paint he could drip down Don's plumber crack onto his undies. He never had a clue until he changed, and each accused the other saying, you were flicking paint at me first when I wasn't looking. Don was sure it was safer in Vietnam. Dad finally filled the pool with dirt and covered it with grass. He said with the boys gone, it was too much work.

Mom was very active in church and the family would go Sunday morning, evening and every Wednesday night. She became the church organist and she couldn't read music. Mom played strictly by ear. I was always impressed by her musical ability. Later, I became the choir director and was even more amazed at her ability to learn new music. All she had to do was here the melody one time and she had it down.

After I was discharged from the Navy, I became a Helicopter and Airplane Pilot. Dad, my brothers Don and Larry started taking flying lessons in a Piper Cherokee airplane that Don had bought. Mom then decided she wanted to learn also.

On one of my return trips from the middle east, mom wanted to show me what she had learned and asked if I would fly with her. We were flying toward the Vincent Thomas Bridge in San Pedro CA when she started a decent to fly under the bridge. I asked what she was doing, and she stated, "I'm going to fly under the bridge I do it all the time. I told her "Not with me onboard I could lose my License". A moment to remember. Dad, Don and Larry continued taking lessons and

Mom

obtained their Pilot License, but Mom never finished her training, (Another story). My other brother Jerry showed no interest in flying.

My Father was the most influential person in my life. He was teaching me everything he could, starting with his trade as an automobile mechanic. When I was discharged from the Navy dad got me a job at Cormier Chevrolet where I worked starting on the Lube Rack. After 1 year he had trained me enough that I was promoted to a line mechanic. I can remember going to work with dad during summer vacations from High School on Saturdays and watching him work. Dad was a Master of all trades and I wish I was more like him.

Another man that greatly influenced me was my Uncle Jess Rector. We were more like 2 kids and always having a ball. We started a model railroad project together and would work way into the night in his garage until we finished the project. We were always looking for something to do.

We would go fishing in his boat on Saturdays and sometimes I would water ski. He would always give it just enough power to get me about halve way up out of the water and drag me all the while laughing hysterically.

I started building remote control airplanes and flying them. My Uncle said he wanted to do it also, so I gave him an old reed control box. He built a beautiful model and was ready for his first flight. I told him to charge the control set for 24 hrs. and then it would be ready for flight. The next morning, we went to the model airport and set up. I took the plane off for him and handed him the controls. After about 2 minutes he stated that the controls were not working and handed them to me. As I tried to get it to work, I asked him how long he had charged the batteries and he stated 3 hours. I handed it to him and said enjoy. When he had the controls in his hand, he said it's still not working, I told him that the batteries were dead. He had a very stupid look on his face that I will never forget. His logic was he only wanted to fly for about 15 minutes and thought that a 3-hour charge would be enough. (Whoops!) One of many great times we had together.

Born and raised in Texas most of the boys wore cowboy clothes and no one thought anything about it.

However, in 1955 my dad moved the family from Wichita Falls Texas to Long Beach California as I turned 13. Arriving as a freshman in Jr High, the only clothes I had were levis, cowboy shirts and boots, everyone knew me as Tex, and I hated this.

As a teenager it is important to have self-esteem and to fit in. So, I signed up as a School Hall Monitor so I could arrive early and change clothes before classes started. There were no cowgirls to date, so it was a long year.

Mom just didn't understand and made all the boy's shirts out of the same material (we looked like poster children). She insisted that all us wear our cowboy clothes, including boots, so I bought clothes and kept them at school in my locker except to wash them. That whole year I was called Tex. It wasn't until my junior year that I lost the nick name and really was included as one of the regular classmates.

Once I had lost the nick name, I was more readily accepted and known by most of the students. This continued all the way through High School, and It has followed me through my career I'm no longer Tex!

Inventions

*I*nventions that had a big impact on my life.

In 1954, my father purchased the first TV in the neighborhood. Wow it was incredible to be able to sit in the living-room on the floor and watch a show. There was only 3 hours each day that there was a broadcast. Every day at 5pm the "Howdy Doody Show" would come on and several of the kids in the area would be there to watch with us. I guess the next was when TV was broadcast in color. It is amazing now to watch the children watching TV, they just take it for granted along with all the other electronical devices at hand.

I believe the greatest impact for me now is the cell phone. I can remember flying home every six months from the middle east and noticing more and more people each trip would have a phone in their ear. I just couldn't believe that so many people could be so important, that they had to have a phone with them all day. Well, when I returned to the USA the last time I too purchased a Cell phone for me and my wife so I could always let her know I had landed and on the way home.

Today I really believe Cell Phones are the downfall of civilization as we knew it. The children of today have lost their skills to communicate, as everything is now texting to their friend sitting right next to them. Nothing seems personable anymore.

On one of my flights thru Tokyo Japan, I was setting in the smoking lounge and noticed a young Japanese girl texting on two phones at the same time. I mentioned it to a gentleman setting next to me and he told me it was his daughter. He then said she was texting in English on 1 phone and Japanese on the other. I was blown away when he told me that. The youth of today with their IPADS, Cell Phones, and all other electrical devices are lost in never-never land.

Anytime you see the students and now adults walking, at a restaurant, and even sometimes trying to drive they are on their Cell phones texting. GOD HELP US!!

1960 First Job as a Drummer

uring my senior year of high school, I was bored and looking for something to do. It was a Friday night, two of my friends and I decided to drive from Long Beach California to downtown Hollywood. As we were passing the intersection of Hollywood and Vine, we heard music coming from a building, and decided to check it out. We entered the building not knowing what was going on inside, but we were curious. On stage were three men singing and playing. We maneuvered ourselves to the front of the stage while watching and listening. After a few songs, I started pulling at the leader's pant leg. He kept looking down at me a little irritated, and finally asked, what do you want? I told him, you only have three guitars, and you need a drummer. He replied, well tell me something I don't know. I said okay, I'm a drummer. Of course, I had never seen a set of drums up close in my life. He said really, can you stick around after the show and we will talk, I replied yes and stood by.

When the show ended, he asked me where I lived, I told him Long Beach. He said great, we live in Torrance, can you audition Thursday night. I said sure no problem and gave him my phone number. I was positive he would never call, but to my surprise the following Tuesday, he called. He gave me his address and said be here at 7:00 PM for the audition. I told him no way he only had a guitar, and I had a full set of drums, if he wanted an audition he'd have to come to my house. Again, very surprised he said, OK.

Now my problem was just starting. In high school woodshop I had made numerous bongos and a few conga drums. I called Gilmour music and ask if they would accept a trade of conga and bongo drums for a full drum set. He said bring them down and we'll see what you've got. The trade was great, and I received a full set of white Pearl drums, along with all the hardware, and symbols. Of course, now that I have a drum set, I don't know how to play them, and I only had two days to learn. Dave a neighbor, taught me how to play the sock symbol rhythm and that was all I could do. With two days to practice, I had the sock symbol rhythm down perfect.

When Thursday night came around my parents said they would leave me alone and went out for the evening. At around 7 PM Bob Burks the leader, and the rest of the group arrived. I guess it was only 20 or 30 minutes later when Danny Florence and the Champs (They recorded the song Tequila) was knocking at my door asking if this was the place. I invited them in, and the jam session started. I guess maybe an hour had passed and Bob said, Ray go ahead and show us what you got. Not knowing what to do I told him when I was ready, he would know it. He backed off and said Okay, OKay.

Towards the end of the evening, Bob looked at me and said, welcome to the group. In total shock I said thank you. He gave me the address of the theater and said to be there tomorrow night by 5 o'clock for rehearsal, because we go on the air live at 7.

After they left, I could not believe I was hired to play drums for a band and going on the radio live tomorrow night. Eventually I convinced myself that I could do it. I arrived at the theater at approximately 4:30 and started setting up my drums. The rest of the band arrived at 5 o'clock and we started playing. Unknown to me, Mickey Finn was their manager, Mickey was a movie star and drummer. After a few songs, Mickey asked me how long I had played the drums. I asked him, what time is it, he laughed and said, no problem Ray you'll be fine, and we will get you through this.

Well, now I'm getting set for the most embarrassing moment of my life. Just before 7 PM a man walked out on the stage and started counting, 5, 4, 3, 2, 1. Good evening ladies and gentlemen, welcome once again to the Celebrity Theater, tonight we have an addition to the Bob Burks Trio, looking and pointing to me he said, OK drummer boy take it away.

For a moment it felt like my heart came out of my chest, as I was grasping for what to do. Because of my Conga and Bongo drum playing experience, almost subconsciously I switched the snare drum over to a tom tom and began a drum solo with my hands. When I finished, I received a standing ovation and Bob Burks said, Wow, Ray when you let go, you let go, good job. Little did I know, this theater was an after-hours Playboy Club.

Well I did learn to play the drums and the band went on to back Debbie Reynolds in two live shows. Our lead singer was drafted, the band broke up and I joined the Navy.

1959 My First Helicopter Flight

was a junior in high school, on a double date in Griffith park in Orange California. It was a great day and we we're having a lot of fun, rowing boats, walking, etc. I had spent all of my money except for $0.50. As I was driving out of the park heading home, I noticed a helicopter making numerous takeoff and landings. I was very curious and stopped to watch. It became obvious that the pilot was giving rides, I approached him and asked how much, he told me $1. I explained to him that I only had $0.50 and could I have a short ride. He said no, because if people saw how short it was, they would not pay a dollar. I then asked how long he would be here, he asked me why and I told him I would drive home to Long Beach, get another $0.50 and come back. He laughed and said you really want to go that bad. I told him yes Sir I do, he replied OK wait over there and when I have only one passenger, I will take you for $0.50. The flight was incredible and immediately I knew I wanted to be a helicopter pilot.

I started taking lessons at a cost of $75 per hour in a Bell 47D model helicopter. My instructor was an active Coast Guard helicopter pilot, looking for extra money on the side. He was not a good instructor and I almost gave up. After eight hours of lessons I still could not hover. He told me I was not coordinated enough to fly helicopters and maybe I should look for another line of work. By paying him $75 per hour I felt I had some say in this matter. We landed, and at the time I was a heavy smoker and decided to have a cigarette and think about what he said. While setting there I noticed a trigger for the first time on the cyclic. I asked when they installed the trigger, he said it's always been there, why. I asked, well, what's it for, he said on some helicopters when you pressed the trigger you can talk on the radio. However, on this helicopter there was only a handheld microphone. I continued smoking my cigarette and convinced myself that if I depressed the trigger the helicopter would dismantle. When I finish my cigarette, I lifted the helicopter into a stationary hover, and the instructor couldn't believe it. I know now that my problem was, I was too tense, had a death grip on the cyclic, and could not feel any movement of the helicopter. In order to relax my grip, I extended my pinky to prevent a strong grip on the cyclic. My instructor never noticed my white knuckles and advised me to relax. As a helicopter instructor now with 54 years' experience, I know this is a very common problem, in the primary stage of learning to fly a helicopter. You must be relaxed in order to feel the error before it occurs.

With about 35 hours flying time, I heard of a new company in Long Beach giving lessons. After investigating I discovered that the Hughes aircraft company was opening a flight school with Hughes H-269 helicopters. They had a program called the 20/20 club. If you purchased 20 hours in advance, the price would be $20 per hour. This new pricing enabled me to complete my training.

Obtaining my pilot certificate was not easy, I managed an apartment house for free rent, bought a car for $50, and after three years of doing without, finally the day came that I had my commercial pilot certificate. I tell the story that my first flight only cost me $0.50, however several thousand dollars later I received my pilots certificate.

At the time I was working at Cormier Chevrolet as an automobile mechanic and every time a helicopter would fly over It made me want to fly even more. One day I decided the only way I would finish my training would be too stop being a mechanic and seek other employment. I gave my father my rollaway toolbox and told him my plan. Dad replied he thought I was crazy as there was no way I could become a pilot. I explained to him that it was my dream and I was going to pursue it. I drove a Jewel T Home Shopping truck enabling me the opportunity to take lessons every day.

After I received my pilot certificate, my brother Don purchased a piper Cherokee 140 to reduce the cost of him learned to fly. My father, two of my brothers, Don, and Larry both obtained their private pilot license. Mom also decided she wanted to get hers and started taking lessons. Jerry, another brother showed no interest in flying. On one of my vacations while at home, mom wanted me to go flying with her. As a student pilot she couldn't take any one with her, so as a pilot I could go. While flying over the Los Angeles Harbor, I noticed she had started a decent toward the Vicente Tomas Bridge. When asked what she was doing, she told me she was going to fly under it. As this is illegal, I told her not with me onboard because I could lose my license. She then told me she did it all the time. By the way, mom never received her license.

Navy

n 1960 I graduated high school in Long Beach CA. During my senior year I had taken several flying lessons because I wanted to be a pilot. As you know by now, I really wanted to fly helicopters, but it was very expensive, so I started with airplanes.

Not knowing what I was going to do I met with a Navy recruiter, about joining the Navy to be a pilot. The recruiter gave me several tests and determined that I had passed, then promised me aviation. To a 17-year-old when he promised me aviation, that had to mean I was going to be a pilot. He gave me instructions to report downtown Los Angeles to be sworn in before going to San Diego for boot camp. I queried him by saying I thought pilots went to Annapolis. He replied they do after going to boot camp. Well the recruiter signed me up and away I went, only he put me on the wrong boat, LOL.

During the eight weeks in boot camp at what they called Hells island, they passed out several flyers for me to decide what I wanted to do in the Navy. Each time I received one I threw it in the trash, because I knew I was going to be a pilot. Week 7 was when we were to tell them our decision. When I met with the Sr. Chief, he asked what I wanted to do. I replied to him Sir I want to be a helicopter pilot. He's stated boy, we don't need any more pilots, so what is your decision? I told him I didn't know, and he told me I had one minute to make a decision are you start eight weeks of Hells island all over again. I told him the recruiter guaranteed me aviation, that's why I didn't look at any of the flyers given to me. Looking me in the eye he stated, aviation, OKAY you look like a good Aviation Boatswains Mate.

After boot camp, I was sent to Philadelphia for Aviation Boatswains Mate Fuel school. The school prepares you to work on an aircraft carrier aviation fuel system. The school was very good and also taught me fire/crash rescue.

The school was during the winter, and as a California boy, I was not used to the cold and snow. One weekend I hitch hiked to Elliot Maine from Philadelphia in the worst snow storm the east coast had seen in many years. I was wearing my Navy Pee coat, and was freezing. A truck driver picked me up and said he was going all the way to Elliot himself. When we arrived in Elliot he said he needed to turn the truck into the yard and then he would drive me to my Uncles house. An unbelievable trip thanks to this unknow man.

When I showed up art my uncles house unannounced Friday night late and he couldn't believe I had hitch hiked. I told him that was the only way I could come and visit him, and I had to leave the next day to go back to the base. Uncle Lewis looked me in the eye and said "Boy I will buy you an airline ticket and drive you to Boston airport Sunday. A visit I will never forget.

1965 First Job as a Pilot

While taking helicopter lessons, my uncle came to visit my mother and father in Long Beach California. He was a sitting judge in Mineral Wells Texas, this was the location of Fort Walters Primary Army Helicopter Training Center. During his visit my dad told him I was taking helicopter lessons and wanted to be a pilot. Uncle Bob, then came to me and told me when I had my license to come and see him as he could obtain a job for me. I asked him how he was able to do that because everywhere I had checked required the pilot to have 1000 hours. He told me he knew the general manager (Mr. Thompson) at Fort Wolters and was sure he could get me a job.

After receiving my Commercial Helicopter Pilot Certificate, I Contacted my uncle and he said I could come down whenever it was convenient for an interview. He told me he had spoken with Mr. Thomas, the general manager and he said for you to come on down when you have your commercial. I was very excited to say the least and had told all of the other students at the training center that I was going to Texas and guaranteed a job. Five of the other pilots asked if they could go with me for an interview. My self and one other pilot were dual rated, both airplane and helicopter so we rented an aero commander 500 airplane and flew to Mineral Wells.

On arrival at Fort Walters we went to the chief standardization pilot's office and ask if they were hiring pilots. He asked how many flight hours did we have , I told him the average was around 250 hours, he laughed and said, son do you see all of the folders in the cabinet, all of the pilot applications in there are in excess of 1000 hours flight time. He suggested maybe we go to Acme truck driving school and apply there. I was devastated along with the animosity of the other pilots with me, it was not a good day. The other pilots we're insisting that we leave immediately and fly home. I told them out of respect for my uncle, at least I had to see Mr. Thomas and thank him for the opportunity. They were not happy and told me to hurry up. I was allowed to see Mr. Thomas almost immediately and he seemed happy to see me. He said that my uncle had spoke highly of me and told of my desire to be a helicopter pilot. He asked if I had my commercial certificate and I told him yes. He then said well congratulations, can you come to work two weeks from today. I was stunned and while stammering a little replied Yes Sir! He asked if the gentlemen in the lobby were with me and I told him yes. He asked if they all had commercial and about the same flight time. I said, yes and he told me to get them and bring them in. I brought them in, and he asked if they could start in two weeks. Talk about an excited group of people. I know that if I hadn't shown respect for my Uncle, we would not have been hired.

When I reported to Fort Walters, the first day there were six fatalities. As you can imagine there was a lot of Chaos. We all started in the M.O.I. class (Method of Instruction) for 8 weeks learning how to teach the Army way. I was assigned to the OH-23 squadron which is a Hiller helicopter. Each morning Mr. MacFarlane, the chief standardization pilot that I had met and was told to try Acme truck driving school, came to the class and asked for a student to train. It was rumored throughout the base that Mr. MacFarlane was the best on the base. Everyone was told that if you drilled a hole in the needle on the Airspeed indicator and placed a wire thru the hole it would never touch the edge of the hole. Because of this I was always the first one to raise my hand. In my mind if he was the best, that's who I wanted to learn from. After a few weeks of training, he asked why I was the only one that would fly with him. I told him of the rumor, he laughed, and said I'm no better than any of the other pilots. He asked me if the wind is calm, and the temperature is 100 plus, would you do zero ground run touchdown autos. I said no. He then said Ray, I'll tell you a secret, to put in your hip pocket. To follow a curriculum sometimes will not work, so never pick the day for the maneuver, pick the maneuver for the day.

When I finished the training, I was taking my army instructor check-ride and failed. Upon landing back at the main helipad, Mr. McFarland was there to greet me, and arms stretched out yelled congratulations and welcome aboard. I told him I had failed the check-ride. He asked why and I started telling him the reason. The check pilot on the way back to the main helipad, after completing the entire check-ride items, gave me an engine failure and asked where I was going to land. We were over a duel sod touchdown area and I said I would land on that pad. He asked where on that pad, and I told him when the helicopter stopped the left front upright part of the left skid would be touching the tire in the middle of the pad. I was very happy because that is exactly where we stopped. He asked me what the highest rotor RPM was attained on the last maneuver. I said in the middle of the green arc. he asked again what the highest rotor RPM was attained on the last maneuver, again I said in the middle of the green. He said OK, we can head on back. As we landed, he told me that I had failed due to division of attention. He wanted me to give him a specific rpm. Mr. McFarland was very upset, called dispatch and requested another helicopter. We took off climb to 1000 feet over the base, he then gave me an engine failure, I entered autorotation, several times during the descent he asked me what your RPM is, I would reply it's in the middle of the green. Upon landing, again with arm stretched out he said welcome aboard, don't worry, the check pilot was being ridiculous.

Each instructor was assigned three students and would fly each of them one hour a day. The training was intense, this was because of the shortage of pilots in Vietnam. The primary course was eight weeks long, and the students  would have half day academics, and half day flying. I had one student whose last name was Johnson that was giving me a problem because he was not progressing. Each time I would give him an engine failure he would not lower collective, and of course that will kill you. On a Friday, I told Mr. Johnson he was restricted to quarters for the weekend, and to get a broom handle, and mop handle and set in a chair. The two handles would replace the cyclic and collective. He was to say aloud emergency and push down on the collective stick. I told him that first thing Monday morning I would fly with him, give him an engine failure, and if he did not lower the collective, he would be washed out of the program and sent to Vietnam as a foot soldier. When Monday morning came, I purposely flew him last. 25 minutes into the flight I slowly rolled off the throttle for his emergency. Mr. Johnson thought his leg had rolled off the throttle and quickly increased the power and recovered while apologizing for his error. I told him good job Mr. Johnson let's go land. I never followed through by giving him another engine failure that day. For some reason he never had the problem again.

A different student while trying to hover would always apply both feet on the pedals at the same time, therefore he was unable to stop a spin. I asked the squadron commander if he had ever had a student with this problem, and if so, what did he do. He looked me in the eye and said Ray, I cannot tell you what to do, but I can tell you what we used to do. He said that he you would draw a circle on his left ankle and every time he would apply both feet with equal pressure, he would kick the ankle. Of course, the student would shout and release the pressure. He said after a few times of kicking the ankle it would be very sore and he could not apply equal pressure thus enabling the ability to stop the spin. It worked after a few kicks.

I was given a student that was set back because of his inability to pass a check-ride. A few flights with the student I quickly understood his problem. We were flying in the traffic pattern and his altitude was erratic. I put my hand on the cyclic and told him to relax, because he was oscillating. He shook the controls and told me not to touch the controls again while he was flying. I said, I HAVE THE CONTROLS. I landed at the base of the tower and shut the helicopter down. This gentleman was never to fly again and transferred off the base.

At the time there we had Vietnamese students, and I had not been assigned one. One afternoon my flight commander came to my desk as said, you haven't had a Vietnamese student yet, so now you have. He gave me a student folder that was about 2 inches thick, a normal folder was ½ to ¾ inches. The student had 97 hours of flight training and could not solo. We were forbidden to fail a Vietnamese because they would lose face and commit suicide. He could fly very well but had a problem with the English language. On each of the practice runways there were 4 panels for landing. When he was instructed to land on the most available upwind panel, he would always make his approach to the most upwind panel for landing whether there was another helicopter on the spot or not. I would ask him didn't you see the helicopter on the panel you were about to land on. He would reply, but you said land on most upwind panel sir. The next day I made a radio call that I was going to solo Mr. Nakatani and all you could hear on the radio was, army 2341 departing, army 9678 departing etc., etc. He did an outstanding job and was signed off as completing his solo. A few mornings later as all the instructors were preparing for the daily one of them yelled, Ray someone is messing with your car. As I approached my car, I could see a shadow lurking around inside the front seat. When I approached, I discovered it was Mr. Nakatani, when asked what he was doing, he replied, sir I have present for you. A 5th of scotch, and a necktie from Vietnam was laying on the front seat. He then stated in my country momma and papa are number One, but sir you are Number One.

After two years of training at Fort Walters, I witnessed a tornado that came through and destroyed several 100 helicopters. The H-300 helicopters at the Downey heliport located on the Mineral Wells airport were all piled in a stack along with two jeeps and a fuel truck. There were C-130s flying in parts 24 hours a day. As the H-300 helicopters started to fly again, almost daily a helicopter would crash as the main rotors would seize up and stop. The base commander would ground all flights until further notice. After two days they would relaunch, stating they needed more pilots in Viet Nam, and the another would crash. After several of these launches, seize, launch, the wives of the instructors marched on the Commanders office and demanded all flights seize until the problem was fixed or their husbands would not fly. The Commander did not listen, and a notice was disseminated among the OH-23 pilots that if they were qualified in the H-300, they would be transitioned Monday morning to the H-300 squadron or be terminated. Of course, I was H-300 qualified and did not want to transition. That Friday I flew to California, took a check-ride with Utility Helicopters in Long Beach, and almost did not get hired. The Chief Pilot asked me to fly out to the oil platform and land on the spot, and each time I would land 3 feet behind. He told me I had a good touch on the controls but kept missing the spot. I realized what he was saying and told him that at Ft Wolters we were instructed to land 3 feet behind the spot. He then told me to try 1 more time, and of course I landed right in the middle of the spot. After being hired I flew back to Mineral Wells, and Monday morning resigned.

I really believe by following the lessons taught to me by my father;

1. Never lie,

2. Always show respect, and

3. Be Kind to others, that this is the only reason I'm a pilot today.

1966 Job in Nicaragua

I had been with utility helicopters about one year, the company had purchased the first Bell Jet Ranger helicopter on the west coast. One afternoon while flying off Huntington Beach California I received word from the office to call. As soon as I landed, I called and was asked if I could come to the office, have a check out in the new Jet Ranger, and leave for Nicaragua in two days. After speaking with my wife, I agreed. The check-out lasted approximately 40 minutes and I was cleared to go.

Two days later I departed for Houston Texas, with only a sectional map, which was common for navigation and those days. In Texas the map shows rivers however, they have not seen water in years. This makes it difficult to navigate using only the map. I was making position checks visually with reference to the map and it appeared I was right on course. I contacted Austin approach control and told them I was approximately 25 miles west, and inbound for landing. The controller gave me two turns for radar identification and started directing me to the airport. I reported the field insight and the controller advise me of an aircraft approaching on my left side and wanted me to report when I had the aircraft insight. When the aircraft never appeared, I advise the controller and he stated that his radarscope covered 50 miles and I was not on it. He asked if I could see a water tower anywhere because in Texas all water towers had the name of the city written on the side. With my luck, the only water tower insight had no name here was a major highway in front of me, so I landed in a clearing located inside of an off ramp. I then walked to a gas station close by and asked how far I was from Austin. He told me I was 55 miles South of Austin on the San Antonio highway. After taking off I gave Austin approach control my location and advised I needed direction to the nearest airport with jet fuel.

They gave me a heading and distance to an airport that reportedly had jet fuel. Upon arrival I was told they had not carried jet fuel for three years. It is allowed to mix avgas with jet fuel for a percentage of engine life. After refueling I departed and was enroute to Austin. On short final I advised the tower I wanted to land at the base of the tower and speak with the controller that had been handling me. The tower operator advised me they had just completed crew change, and everyone had left. Well, so much for letting the controller know he needed to be more specific when he identified an aircraft by radar. They rest of the flight was uneventful and I landed on the jack-up platform and secured it for getting underway.

After Five days at sea, the captain called me too his quarters and said, prepare to leave the platform and fly to Puerto Cabezas 220 nautical miles away. I asked if he had any aviation maps, he replied that he did not and would take a fix with a Sexton give me a heading. I departed the platform and after flying approximately 20 minutes I started encountering numerous rain squall lines. The overall flight would take about two hours and I knew that when I arrived at the shoreline, I would not know which way to turn. With this in mind I did a 5-degree course correction to the right. Now on arrival at the shore I would turn left. The captain had told me it would be easy to recognize Puerto Cabezas because it had a pier and an airport. After turning to the left and flying 25 minutes I saw a pier that was maybe 50 feet long, and a PBY airplane setting in what looked like a cow pasture, of course this was the airport. Not knowing for sure if this was Puerto Cabezas, when I landed, I kept the RPM at 100%. There were 2 jeeps approaching with armed soldiers and came very close to the helicopter. I opened my window and ask the question, is this Puerto Cabezas. To my relief, they replied yes, so I shut the engine off, I had arrived.

Puerto Cabezas, as you may or may not know was the launching point for the US Bay of Pigs invasion, that is why they had U.S. military jeeps and various other U.S. equipment. The runway was all but destroyed because being the only paved surface in the village, they would drive their halftracks up and down the runway.

The heliport was the president of Nicaragua's vacation home and we used his tennis court. Each day after flying, the villagers single file, would walk by and kiss the helicopter.

On the third week of flying, enroute to the platform I could smell a funny smell. I asked if anyone was smoking and no one was. All of a sudden, the flight controls started jerking and became very stiff, now it was obvious that the smell was hot hydraulic fluid. The passenger in the left seat was a very large man and I ask him if he had ever flown a helicopter before. Of course, he stated no, and I told him I was going to give him his first lesson. I said when I tell you push this stick down as hard as you can. I knew if I could not land on the platform I would have to ditch in the water. When we arrived over the platform, I told the man, now push the stick down. We landed and it appeared to be a normal landing. After checking the problem, I found one of the hydraulic lines had a small hole and was spraying oil onto the hot engine. An engineer on the platform fabricated a new line and filled the reservoir with hydraulic fluid. All is well, that ends well.

There were probably 50 to 60 bars in the village leftover from when the military was there for the invasion. The village only had a population of around 300 people. Each night after work we would all jump into a company pickup truck and start looking for which bar, we would have a drink. The villagers would follow the truck, and that would be the bar of the night. Alcohol was not the best because the rum was three days old and the beer two weeks old.

This is when and where I acquired the taste and learned to drink Scotch. One afternoon a German freighter had arrived with supplies for the village and the base manager purchased 2 cases of White Horse Scotch and 5 cases of Tuborg beer. Each night at dinner they would pour everyone a Scotch and water. I would take a sip and then dump in the sink. The taste was like iodine. Each night I would sip a little more before pouring it out. On the 7th night they ask if I would like another glass, and I replied maybe just half, I have to fly tomorrow. Since that night, Scotch has been my preferred drink.

1968 Mt Potosi

n the outskirts of Las Vegas Nevada is a mountain called Mt. Potosi. The elevation of Mt. Potosi is 8,500 feet. On the summit of the mountain is where Carole Lombard crashed. There are still pieces of the aircraft scattered on the mountain. I was hired to sling load and set a TV repeater tower on the summit for communications. At the time I was living in Long Beach California and had a company that was hired to do the job. I flew there early morning and set up for the lift, it was a clear day, and the wind was calm. I started the lift from the desert floor, and it took a while climbing to altitude. Upon reaching the summit I position the tower over the hole and started lowering it.

As the Tower lowered into the hole, the waste gate on the turbo charger for the Bell G3B1 helicopter failed, reducing power on the engine to idle. At this time there was nothing I could do other than release the load and dive the aircraft to clear the now standing tower.

The helicopter contacted the ground on a 45° down slope and started sliding down the mountain towards the edge. There was one tree between me, and a 2000-foot drop and I hit it dead center. When everything stopped and the dust settled, I was sitting in the cockpit with no doors or bubble, it was just me. At the time I was a heavy smoker and reached for my pack of Marlboro. It appears that my cigarettes went over the side with the other pieces of the aircraft. I looked back up the hill and my crew were running down the hill to me thinking I was dead. I yelled, "Slow down, and look for my cigarettes". The only injury was one of the crew started laughing and tripped, fell and had a scratch on his left arm. I was very, very lucky to say the least. Several hours later I was in the terminal at the Las Vegas McCarran airport having a cup of coffee waiting to board my flight home and looked out the window, there was Mt. Potosi and realizing what it happened I went into shock. It took about 30 minutes to regain my composure. The next day in the office talking to the mechanic I explained what had happened. The mechanic said he wasn't surprised because the wastegate had been failing intermittently. When he said this, I remember punching him and as he lay on the floor, I couldn't believe he had not repaired the wastegate or at least made note and advised anyone.

1969 M*A*S*H

Everyday driving from Long Beach California, to Whiteman Airport in San Fernando Valley, I would pass by the 20th Century Fox studios. One day out of boredom from the drive, I decided to stop and see if they needed any stunt pilots. Upon arrival at the studio I drove onto the lot, up to a building, and entered unchallenged. I walked down the hall where I found an office for Mr. Mark Evans, a junior producer. I said good morning introduced myself and asked if he needed any stunt pilots. He replied who are you, and how did you get in here, I chuckled and said I walked. He looked at me and said well walk yourself back out of here. With that response I left the building, I can remember laughing most of the remaining drive to work that day.

Approximately 2 weeks later while driving to work I couldn't resist it. Upon arrival at fox studios again unchallenged, I found my way to Mr. Evans office. This time I ask if he needed any stunt pilots yet, he looked up and said you again, how did you get in here? I replied again, I walked. His message was very clear this time, "WELL WALK YOURSELF RIGHT BACK OUT OF HERE."

I guess by now four or five weeks have passed and again driving to work I just couldn't resist. As I entered Mr. Evans office he looked up and said, where have you been? I was shocked at his response and said I've been flying. He asked if I still wanted to be a stunt pilot. Of course, I replied "Yes Sir". He then stated that 20th century was almost bankrupt after the production of Hello Dolly, and they were going to make a movie just to keep the crews busy. None of the stars were known actors and the only way they could lose money was if they lost the can of film. The name of the movie was M*A*S*H.

He then asked if I could obtain a Korean War vintage helicopter, I replied, Sir I own three of them. He asked for my telephone number and said he would call me to make all arrangements. Of course, I  thought this was just another way to get rid of me. However, to my surprise I received a phone call and asked if they could come and paint the helicopter for the movie. Mark and I became good friends, I had his personal cell phone number, and later he became an executive producer for 20th Century.

The day finally came that I was asked to report to the Fox Ranch for filming. At the time, National Helicopters had control of all helicopter flying for movies. Two gentlemen from National arrived on the set and started telling the producer and director they were making a mistake by using me as the pilot because I was not a seasoned actor. The conversation went on for about 45 minutes and finally the director looked at me and said, "Ray can you do this?" I replied, "Yes Sir, no problem.'" The director instructed his people to show those two gentlemen off the set.

For four days we filmed the helicopter scenes and on the 4th day I was given the task of dropping a net full of garbage on the character Frank while he was setting in a Jeep. The winds in Malibu Canyon, (which is the location of the Fox Ranch), sometimes can be very challenging for precision flying. After about 2 hours of trying to drop the garbage on Frank because the wind kept changing direction, the director said Ray thank you for the effort you've put forth, I'm giving you a $3,000.00 bonus and we'll finish the shot with a crane off camera.

9-17-1972

About two years had passed when I received a call from Mr. Evans, he stated that CBS was interested in making a Pilot for the TV show M*A*S*H, and would I be able to do it. He asked if I was a member of the

ADAMS RIBS

Screen Actors Guild. I told him no, he then said I needed to join because, I had already worked under the Taft Hartley Act. He told me I could join under the must join clause and it would cost approximately $800. I told him no, I did not want to spend $800. He became quite insistent that I join and said it would pay me back 100-fold. To this day I am so glad I joined.

Gary Burghoff, (Radar) and I were the only two from the cast that came from the Movie to the TV Series. I played the character Dangerous Dan the Helicopter Pilot, any time they needed help they would tell Radar to get Dan. I flew all the Helicopter Scenes and even flew

5 O'CLOCK CHARLIE

the airplane in the episode 5 o'clock Charlie

While shooting the series

There was a scene Where an orphaned boy had wandered into a minefield. The script called for Dan to fly Trapper over the orphan and lift him to safety.

When I arrived, the director while winking at me said, "Ray when did you get out of the hospital? That was a bad crash? I went Along, and told him about two weeks ago. He walked me back and started laying out the scene he wanted. At this time, he introduced me to a young man, (not a stuntman) that was going to be the stunt double for Hawkeye. He described the scene that I would fly the stuntman into position and lift the child stuntman from the minefield and return to a clear area. Understanding the scene that the director wanted, I proceeded too brief the acting stuntman. I Ask him how long he had been a stuntman, he replied that he was not a stuntman and the director offered him $100.00 to do this stunt. I laid out the 50-foot cable that he would be attached to and briefed him what to do if there was a problem. I told him that if I had to put him on the ground not to move but to lay flat on the ground and I would move the helicopter to the right and land. I then showed him a little red button on my controls and told him that if I pushed the red button it would release the cable. He looked concerned and asked me about how high I would be lifting him off the ground. I told him just a few feet. Of course, for the angle the director wanted would require me to lift him approximately 100 feet off the ground. After the shot was complete, I set him on the ground, moved to the right and released the cable. Once I had landed and shut down, I noticed the stuntman was still standing, holding the cable, and looking straight up. I walked over and ask if he was OK, he said yes Sir, I'm fine I think, I was just thinking about that little red button.

Another memorable scene for me was a shot where I was lowering a stuntman doubling Hawkeye into a foxhole on a hill to perform emergency surgery in the field. He had been at a Christmas party dressed as

Santa. As the stuntman was almost on the ground, a large explosion was set off close by. They forgot to brief me about this, and it totally took me by surprise.

Filming the movie was quite different. The principle actors, Don Southern and Elliot Gould were very Obnoxious and stuck up. Maybe it was because it was their first leading role in a motion picture, and they were caught up with themselves. I had very little contact with them, and that was fine with me. As you know there are two helicopters in the opening scene. I am the second one and directing the scene.

Each time there was a character change, they would re-shoot the opening on the helipad and tie the shots together. This of course increased the residuals as I found out much later.

After the series ended, one afternoon while living in Las

ALAN ALDA

Vegas, I received a phone call from Alan Alda, and he told me he was in Vegas at Caesar's Palace. He said that the hotel had made a M*A*S*H set in one of the ball rooms and had made a duplication of the SWAMP.

He was launching a new brand of VODKA called, M*A*S*H 4077th Vodka, made from Hawkeye Distilleries. He said to come on down see him and he would give me a sample. I did, see picture, along with one of the bombs from 5 o'clock Charlie.

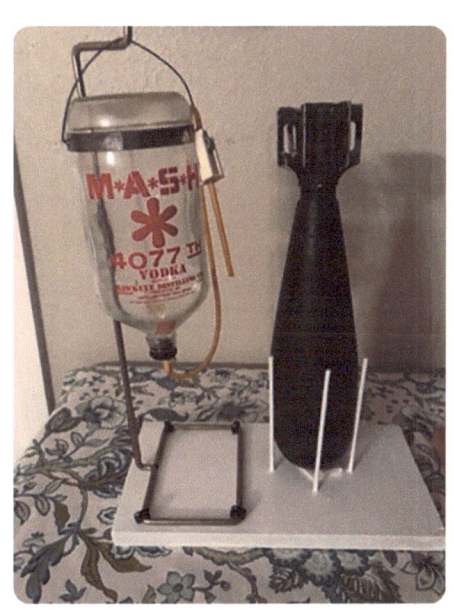

Vodka Bottle

Alan also directed several of the shows and I always enjoyed working with him. Most directors would tell you do this, do that, really not knowing anything new to try or do. Alan would approach each of the key personnel involved in the shot he was looking for and ask, this is what I'm looking for how would you do it. After discussing what our ideas were, we would shoot the scene

Each time a main character was changed, I thought the series would take a hit. When McLean Stevenson left, and Henry Morgan came on the show, it was a surprising boost for the show. Henry was an incredible addition to the cast and very well received by all.

McClean

McLean was an extremely funny person to be around. Every time the director would say cut, Mac would start an extemporaneous dialog that would break up the cast. He would continue until the director would say action. Also, at this time I had a contract at the PORT'S O CALL village in the Los Angeles Harbor giving helicopter rides. One Sunday afternoon, Mac showed up with his daughter and we took her for a helicopter ride. The appearance of McLean (Star of M*A*S*H) was like a magnet, sucking all the tourist to the heliport. After Mac and daughter left, the line of people that had bought tickets to ride on the same helicopter that he had been on, was hours long. No one knew that I was the M*A*S*H pilot, and this was the M*A*S*H helicopter. Mac was gracious and said he would bring his daughter every Sunday and go for a ride if it would help. Thank you, MAC. When Mclean was leaving the show, the writers rewrote the ending of the show. Unknown to anyone until the show aired. While at the cast party, they called Gary off to the side and reshot the ending where the news reporting that Mac was killed in a plane crash while on his way home from Korea.

Next Wayne Rogers left to return to his private business and handle the financial affairs of numerous actors in Hollywood. He was replaced by Mike Farrell. Mike came to visit the set of a show we were shooting, just before replacing Wayne, and brought his wife and all of his children. I let

Alan, Mike Farrell & Me

them climb all over the helicopter and they had a great time.

Loretta Swit, I believe always showed up on the set-in character. My wife had bought a hard-back cover of M*A*S*H and asked me to have it autographed. One day the cast were all sitting in a circle going over lines, and I felt this would be a good time to get the signatures. Radar was sitting next to me, so I asked him first for his autograph and explained it was for my wife. He said no problem Ray, and I'll pass it around when I'm finished. As it was passed around and everyone was signing, Larry Linville had signed it and offered it to Loretta. She asked Larry (Frank), what is this. He told her it was for my wife. She said very harshly, I don't have time for that. Larry, then said, "Sign it Hot Lips", she looked him in his eyes and said very sweetly, Okay Frank. From that moment on, I believed she was type casted.

Gary Burghoff, (Radar) was a very quiet person, but a lot of fun to work with. Later after the series ended, Gary moved to the mountains and became a recluse.

The cast of the TV show were great to work with and a very enjoyable 11 years.

1971 Tuna Boats

As owner of West Coast helicopters, I had supplied several pilots for tuna boats. When I sold my company, I was looking out of my office window trying to decide what I would do next. Then remembering the tuna boat industry, I contacted Apollo fisheries in San Diego, and I explained to them that I had started a company called Aerial Spotters. and was prepared to offer full service for tuna boats with regards to a helicopter, pilots, mechanics and spare parts.

Apollo fisheries set a meeting with a tuna boat owner to explain my service. Upon completion of my Presentation, the owner of the tuna boat stated he wasn't interested in the full service because he wanted to buy the helicopter. For a moment I didn't know what to do, and then it hit me to present a partial service, with just the Pilot, Mechanic and spare parts. I explained that the service included if he did not want a particular pilot or mechanic, that I would meet the boat at the next port o" call with a replacement. His face lit up and said that he wanted this service.

I charged $20.00 per ton which the average boat carried 1200 tons. The average time at sea to get a full load of tuna was one month.

I decided to go on the first trip with the boat for a firsthand feeling for the job. For several days we would spot porpoise, but no tuna. My Captain did not speak English, and of course I did not speak Spanish. We communicated thru the 1st mate onboard the boat.

One afternoon after spotting porpoise with no fish, I asked the 1st mate to tell the Captain I would like to take a closer look at the porpoise if he didn't mind. The captain gave permission and I went very low to the water and started herding the porpoise. As they started moving faster, the tuna came to the surface and the Captain went crazy, he kept saying Piscar, Piscar (fish, fish). We captured 35 tons of tuna on that sighting. That night at the dinner table the Captain acknowledged the helicopter and named it speed boat number one. He told me that if I wanted to try anything else, to just do it, but if it didn't work, not to do it again.

Before the helicopter, they would use speed boats to herd the porpoise by surrounding them and keep them in the net. Now with the helicopter it was easier and faster to control the fish. I was Able to spot porpoise 20 miles away and herd them towards the boat, while the boat was enroute to us. The Captain would have me cut the porpoise from the herd that was carrying the tuna, while the boat surrounded then with the net. The same technique was applied as if you were herding horses.

My company grew rather quickly and within one year I had purchased and paid for 18 helicopters.

Training the Pilots before departing for the boat was the key for success. I would take them offshore between Long Beach California and Catalina Island. We would spot porpoise, teach them to herd, turn, and stop the fish. Also, I had them land on the open ocean, shutdown and restart the engine. I also had them practice emergency autorotation's (Engine OFF Landings) to the water. I learned tuna boat Spanish, i.e. counting so, I could tell the crew the tonnage upon landing.

I would travel and accompany the crews to their first boat, usually in Panama, and introduce them to their Captain. The boat would pull out to sea, and I would fly with them to do ship-board take-offs and landings underway until they were very comfortable. Then have then fly me back to shore and wish them a quick trip.

Living on the boat was 1st class as you had your own state room, meals were excellent, and you were an officer on the boat. I would brief them as to the series of events their mind would go thru.

1. The first 2 weeks are great because everything is new.

2. After the second week you start to get restless.

3. You start to enjoy the trip and understand when the boat's full, you will return.

4. However, when you are pulling back into port, you do not want to get off the boat.

I never had to exchange, a crew for any Captain. After a while the Captains started requesting that the crews stay onboard for a back to back trip, and they would pay me a bonus. I told the Captains to ask the Pilots directly and if they agreed, to pay them. These boats were referred to as bonus boats. I have always believed that if you take care of your people, they will take care of you. With this said, I never had any personnel quit.

It is an unbelievable sight to see 20,000 porpoises, running thru the water. The Tuna experience is truly one I will never forget.

1979 Fire Fighting

was living in Las Vegas Nevada. I started flying on fires and could not believe how fast the desert could burn. The Sage Brush will burn and travel very fast across the desert. While flying under contract with the bureau of land management (BLM), I flew on desert fires, and tall tree fires in the mountains surrounding Las Vegas. Flying a Hughes 500 helicopter with a Bambi Bucket. I would load the Bambi Bucket with either red slurry or water. Flying on fires is very enjoyable and at the same time very stressful.

To get away and relax I bought a boat and kept it at the Lake Mead Marina. On weekends I would try and go there with the family and relax, however I had a Marine band radio on my boat and would always notify the park rangers of the location I would be at in case of an emergency. It never failed as the camp was set up and ready to relax the park rangers would come to the campground by boat and say BLM request your service.

When I would arrive at the fire camp I would always get a big smile on my face when they said, "Ray, get your bucket ready". It's like making bombing runs all day. On several of the fires the terrain was very steep and would not allow men to fight the fire on the ground. I would lay down a line of slurry around the fire for control and eventually, obtained the nickname of Rembrandt.

Sometimes the flames would be over 200 feet high and the heat was incredible. The danger is that if you have an emergency in the air, where do you land. On two different occasions I had emergencies occur. The first one was engine failure, and I was able to land outside the fire line. The second one did not turn out as well. I had been flying on a fire for three days and the fire was all but out. I was preparing to fly back home when the fire boss came to me and stated there was one tree smoldering in the middle of the fire and ask if I could make one more run with water, then he could report the fire was out. I agreed and started an approach for my final run. The flight path took me to the ridge that was the sheer wall about 400 feet high and the other side at 70° down slope. My intention was to come over the ridge and start a decent to make the water drop on the tree about halfway down the hill. As I approach the rim, I had a low side governor failure which brought the jet engine to idle and having no choice at this point I was going to land. With a quick survey looking to both sides I saw one Pinyon Juniper tree and decided that was where I was going to land/crash.

I was able to limp the helicopter over to the tree and as it contacted the tree, the right skid hung up in tree, the helicopter rolled over and came to rest inverted. There were four convict firefighters close by and started to run away as one of the men was yelling, "get back it's going to blow". I yelled back, "you watch too many movies", and one of the men came to my rescue. With the aircraft inverted my shoulder harness was held tight by my weight and I could not release it. The man lifted me up, and I was able to release the harness and get out. I told him how much I appreciated the effort he had made, and he stated "we're even". I ask what he meant, and he asked me if I remembered a fire the previous year by Lake Mead when there was four men trapped in the middle of the fire and they asked for a volunteer to try and get them out. I told him, "yes, I was the pilot that volunteered", and he replied, "I know, I was one of the men that was trapped thank you, we're even now". I told him no we're not and asked how much longer before he would be released. He said, "if the fire season continues maybe six more months". I gave him my phone number and told him when he was released to call me, and I would buy him the biggest steak we could find in Las Vegas. A little more than six months later he called, and we had a great steak dinner.

This was the last fire that I flew on for many years. I told the fire boss that I was giving him my helmet and flight suit and to give it to a younger man and let him have all the fun.

1980 MGM
Grand Fire

I t was early morning, [and] I was at home relaxing and enjoying a coffee in my living room and getting ready to leave for a flight to the Grand Canyon. I was going to film a documentary on the Grand Canyon itself. Just before I left that morning, I received a phone call from the Las Vegas metro Police Department saying Sergeant Harry Christopher, (chief pilot for Las Vegas Metro Police,) requests assistance at The MGM Grand Hotel as it was on fire. I opened my front door and look towards the Las Vegas Strip and I could see the smoke bellowing several thousand feet into the air. I believe it was only approximately [15] fifteen minutes before I arrived at the hotel.

Talking with Harry on the radio, we agreed to start an orbit over the roof evacuating survivors.

The smoke was very thick and toxic, we would take a deep breath before entering the smoke for landing on the roof. At first there [was] were over a hundred [100] people on the roof panicking. Harry had dropped off his police observer on the roof for crowd control and had his hands full and at one point had to draw his weapon to keep them back. They were bringing their luggage and trying to load it on the helicopter, but as they put it on, we threw it out the other side. Ready for takeoff we would inhale deeply, advising the passengers to do the same, and lift off from the roof [dropping rapidly the 20 stories to the parking lot/plaza, where police officers unloaded the passengers and escorted them to safety. This continued for several hours, and only became more challenging as the fire and smoke continually increased.

As the day progressed, the situation grew ever more frantic and hectic. I remember hovering just outside the column of smoke waiting for Harry to take off when I noticed people screaming and waving just  beyond my rotor blades from their windows. Smoke was billowing from their window. I was horrified to see a man suddenly jump from the window falling to certain death. I realized the heat was becoming too much to handle as I witnessed one after another jumping to their death rather than burning alive.

At one point during the rescue the fire department, which we're staging in front of the hotel as our rescue was staging in the rear, called the Police Department requesting

they tell the civilian helicopters to leave the area as they were interfering with their communications. It seemed obvious they had no idea what was taking place at that point.

In the middle of the rescue another helicopter flew thru the smoke just missing my aircraft and circled, and asked us if we needed any assistance. We told him yes, please flyto Bull Head City and pick-up emergency breathing apparatus. Bull Head City was about a 45 Minute flight each way, so we knew it would keep him clear of the rescue. We recognized the helicopter and knew the pilot and his qualifications, and did not want him around, he acknowledged and left for Bull Head City.

In a way, Harry and I were very lucky because we both had flown a job reroofing The MGM Grand Hotel two months prior and knew where all the obstacles were. At rescue's end, we were very gratified our rooftop rescue efforts paid off with the final count of lives saved, Harry and I had rescued 305 people from the MGM Grand Hotel rooftop.

The rescue was winding down when the Air Force helicopter arrived. The reason for their delay was they had to wait for their camera crew before they could depart.

About one month after The MGM Grand Hotel fire, I received a phone call from the producer of the TV show *That's Incredible*. He asked me if I was one of the pilots that had flown [on] the MGM Grand Hotel fire. I told him 'Yes Sir, may I help you? After a few moments discussing the rescue, he asked me if I had any video. When I told him no, he said Oh well, disregard the phone call without any video I can't use you. I guess he then contacted the Air Force as they did have video. However, when the Air Force finally arrived at the scene that morning, there was no smoke and the rescue was all but finished. The Air Force had a video of them lifting one person from a balcony which aired on an episode for the show. That's Incredible. The TV show flew the Air Force flight crew to Hollywood to be in that episode. The President of the United States flew the Air Force crew To Washington and on to the White House, so that the President could thank them personally.

Known to only a few, four months later the Las Vegas Hilton was set ablaze by an arson. I was shopping at Walmart when over the P.A. I heard Ray Poss, you have an emergency phone call. Again, it was the metro police dispatcher requesting my assistance for the Hilton Hotel fire. My daughter had told them where I was. I drove straight to the airport and was at the Hilton within a few minutes. Still suffering from The MGM experience, I was terrified on arrival. At the MGM fire all I ever saw was smoke never a flame.

But now at the Hilton flames were visible from the 7th floor traveling upward to the roof. The metro helicopter was already on scene and when I arrived started directing me where to land on the roof to evacuate people. The metro helicopter this time was hovering to keep the area clear of other aircraft. There were five or six helicopters that had landed in the parking lot and metro had told them to stand by. The personnel I was airlifting we're mostly injured firefighters, however, I did transport Mrs. Hilton from the roof. Triage had been established at the base of the hotel for rapid assessment, treatment, and transport.

Approximately an hour and 20 minutes had passed when the Air Force helicopter arrived. They apologize for being late, but they had to wait on their camera crew. Their first landing on the roof landed on a lightning rod and punctured their fuel tank. As fuel started running onto the roof they lifted and departed. Probably not politically correct, I keyed my mic and said, "THAT'S INCREDIBLE".

Maybe five or six months past and Sergeant Christopher called me and ask what I was doing that afternoon. I told him I had a flight out to Arizona and would return about 1 o'clock. He said the chief of police would like to see me in his office and I had permission to land on the roof at City Hall. I asked Harry what was this all about, and he said the chief wanted to give me a certificate of appreciation for the efforts put forth on The MGM and Las Vegas Hilton hotel fires. He wanted to know if I could be there at 1 o'clock, I told him no problem. Harry told me he was contacting K.L.A.S. channel 8 news and advising them. I arrived at city hall a little before 1pm and the secretary showed me to the chief's office. When I entered, the chief handed me a piece of paper and stated, good job Ray, thanks. As I started to leave, his secretary told him that channel 8 news was here for the certificate awarding ceremony. The chief Grabbed the certificate from my hand and said show them in. He told them they had arrived just in time as he was about to present the certificate. Well with all the pomp and circumstance making this politically correct, I was presented once again the certificate.

I truly understand Las Vegas being an Air Force town, no one wanted to make the Air Force look bad. But sometimes I feel they take it just a little too far. That being said, it truly is a good title, "That's Incredible".

It was twelve years after [the] The MGM Grand Hotel fires that I was able to speak of them without crying. I will never forget people jumping to their deaths and still feel guilty I could not save them. Focusing on the 305 lives Harry and I rescued is the only way I began to overcome that helpless feeling. I realized, in a way, their sacrifice was the strongest motivation to me during the rescue, as I could not stand the thought of seeing anyone else die without a maximum effort to save them.

Harry, bless his heart had the same problem. Harry, still living in Las Vegas was contacted each year on the anniversary of The MGM Grand Hotel fire by a reporter from the Las Vegas Sun newspaper, doing a follow up on fire wanting an interview. Harry always told them he was too busy and to please contact Ray Poss.

Living and working in Point Barrow Alaska, I would receive the calls and reluctantly start to answer their questions but would have to cut the interview short because I would start crying. I was dating Pam, [which] who later became my wife, and when moving my belongings into her condo she saw a photograph [. The photograph was] presented to me by EG and G, a government contracting company that had filmed the entire fire sequence at The MGM Grand. The photo showed my helicopter hovering before entering the smoke on the roof. She asked me, what is this photograph, I told her [,] (just hold that thought and I'll tell you in a moment). We went inside from the garage, sat on the couch, and I said, 'now about that photo', and I started crying like a baby and couldn't stop.

One lazy afternoon on the Las Vegas Strip, several pilots were having coffee. Sgt. Harry Christopher, Donald Usher (Helicopter Pilot on the Potomac River Air Florida flight), myself and a few Vietnam pilots. We were discussing different events that had affected us, when we all broke into tears. It is very hard to explain to someone that has never experienced it. It is buried so deep inside and hidden from yourself and everyone else. I know now, too late, that I should have sought counseling.

I had taken a job in Mexico, and Pam and I we're driving to Mexico City through Roswell New Mexico. On arrival in Roswell we were visiting my aunt and uncle. Lou, my aunt told me that a lady was on her way over to see me. I asked her what about, she'll tell you when she gets here. When the lady arrived, she was beside herself, almost in tears she gave me a big hug and said 'It's taken far to long for me to thank you.' I replied, 'I don't know what you are talking about.' She said, 'I'm sorry, I know you don't remember me but, I was one of the people you rescued from the roof of The MGM Grand Hotel fire.' Never looking for acknowledgement for the rescue, it was very rewarding to hear those two words, *thank you*! It made the 305 lives personal, and again I thought of those who died that had inspired me not to give up.

1987 Sammy Davis Jr.

*I*n 1981 I ran a helicopter service in Las Vegas. I had a heliport located at the Hacienda hotel on the Las Vegas Strip. Several of the major hotels utilized our service to entertain their high rollers. Normally we were asked to take the high rollers on a trip to the Grand Canyon, this would take a little over two hours, and return them back to the heliport where a hotel limousine would take them to their hotel, and they could start gambling fresh again. The Jerry Lewis telethon was in progress at the time, and Sammy Davis Jr. had donated a ring for auction. The Caesars Palace hotel contacted me and asked if I would fly Mr. Davis to the Nellis Air Force Base as the Thunderbirds we're going to make him an honorary member and give him a flight. I agreed and we set the time for departure. Sammy Davis, his bodyguard, and female companion all arrived on time. The bodyguard came to me and said quickly, please tell Sammy there is no room for me on the aircraft and I would drive. I told him no Sir, there's plenty of room and he decided that he would tell Sammy Davis there was no room for him, and he would drive anyway. Mr. Davis was not very happy, boarded the helicopter with his female companion and we left for the Air Force Base. On arrival Mr. Davis was met by the base commander, the Thunderbird pilots, and about 100 other Air-Force personnel. They gave him a tour of the base and returned back to the flight-line to prepare him for his flight. As he was being situated in the cockpit, he was instructed not to touch a handle in the cockpit, he asked why, and was told that was the ejection lever. He asked what you mean ejection, what happens if I pull the lever. They told him a rocket would fire, lifting him and the seat from the cockpit and a parachute would then deploy bringing him back to the earth. Mr. Davis immediately exited the cockpit and said no way am I going, thank you anyway.

I was standing off to the side waiting for the completion of his tour when a reporter from the Las Vegas Sun Newspaper that I knew, approached me and asked if he could fly back to the Hacienda hotel with us when we departed. I told him, we have the room, but I would have to get Mr. Davis's approval. I approached Mr. Davis and ask if the reporter could fly back with us, and he became very upset as to why I could carry another passenger, when there was no room for his bodyguard. I explained that I had told the bodyguard there was plenty of room for him, but he was afraid to fly. Of course, I was embarrassed by his outrage to me in front of the entourage and explained to him there was no problem. "It was very clear Mr. Davis wanted me to follow his instructions exactly and do whatever he told me to, and obviously still pissed I did not somehow persuade his driver to board the chopper."

When his tour was complete, all goodbyes were said, Mr. Davis approached the helicopter. I loaded him and the female companion on board closed the doors and started the helicopter. Mr. Davis was wearing a military flight suit over his street clothes and a Thunder Bird Ascot around his neck. The temperature at the time was approximately 105 degrees Fahrenheit. With doors closed and the cockpit approaching temperatures that would bake a human, I sat there with the engines running, all doors and windows closed, for approximately 15 minutes. I was soaked with sweat, and looking at Mr. Davis, the pomade from his hair was starting to melt and run down his face. Finally, he asked me how much longer before we would take off, I replied, anytime you're ready Mr. Davis. He looked at me, smiled, and said, whoops, you got me.

I guess the moral of this story is, ALWAYS BE NICE TO YOUR PILOT.

1982 Nevada Test Site

*I*n 1982 I was flying for EG&G, this company supported the department of energy. I was hired as the chief pilot for airborne security for the Nevada Test Site. Our primary job was to patrol the Test Site looking for intruders and respond to electronic surveillance alarms. On days of an underground atomic or nuclear test, we would escort the device after it had been spun up and armed for detonation, to the underground test site and lowered into the ground. Just before detonation my job was to patrol the area with 4-armed crewmen for security of the location. We would stay on station until approximately 30 minutes after detonation, looking for hazardous radiation venting from the collapsed detonation sites. If none were detected, we would be released. I witnessed around 50 detonations in all.

Sedan Crater

The Sedan Crater was the only explosion that was designed to blow outward. They used this test to see if they would be able to dig a canal using underground bombs. On the westside of the test site, they exploded 3 underground tests in a row to make a test Canal and the depth from one end to the other was only off less than an inch.

I remember when we first arrived with the helicopter at the Nevada test site, I had designated our call sign as Eagle One. for approximately four months, all flying over the Nevada test site and around the top-secret base known as area 51, we were using the callsign eagle 1. When approaching area 51 we would be queried on the radio as aircraft flying heading 360 degrees identify yourself. We would always respond this is eagle one, and they would respond good evening Sir, have a nice flight. At the end of the fourth month, one evening while on patrol, again we were asked, aircraft flying heading 360 degrees identify yourself. Of course, I responded, this is Eagle One. This time their response was quite different. They stated eagle one is already flying identify yourself. I told them this was the security helicopter for the Nevada Test Site, and they said Roger, eagle one is the commanding officer's call sign for area 51, we suggest you have a new callsign. I thought for a moment and said roger, this is Dragon One, and that callsign remained in effect for the duration.

One evening while setting at our designated heliport, one of the security forces pulled up, got out, and was carrying what looked to me like binoculars. I asked what they were, and he stated they were, tank driver night vision goggles. I ask if I could look through them and could not believe how everything was illuminated. After he left, I ordered four pairs and started experimenting by flying with a safety pilot. The safety aspect of our mission with security of the test site in the darkest of nights was increased by tenfold. I begin training the other pilots and it was not very long until all night flights were performed with night vision goggles.

A training exercise had been set up with the 160th and Delta Force. The officer in charge asked me if I had much experience using Night Vision Goggles. I told him yes and he wanted to know how fast we flew with them, I told him 120 knots. He asked if I was kidding and I said no Sir, that is as fast as our helicopter can go. He was shocked and said that his unit was there to try and increase their speed to 45 knots. He wanted us to follow behind and observe how they would attack a roof top insertion, and then we could do one and debrief. I told him we were civilians and I was afraid my pilots would cheat. I wanted to go first and then he could tell us how to improve our tactics. We did go first and after the flight he wanted to see me in private in my office. He wanted to know how and where we learned the tactics we used as they were exactly like his unit would have done it. I told him just sitting around an open fire discussing options and told him that the Vietnam tactics didn't work. He agreed and our credibility was up considerably. Later I went for a ride with him in their helicopter and at 40 knots my stomach was in my throat as there was no moon or star light to help navigate. When we finished, I asked him if he wanted to fly with me in our helicopter. His answer of course was yes. As we started flying, he said you were joking about flying at 120 knots right. I told him to push a button on the box in front of him. As he did a 10,000,000-candle powered SX-15 search light came on and I increased to 120knots. He couldn't believe his eyes. 1 year later upon his return to the test site, two of his helicopters had the same search light.

At the test site, I saw many strange things. One Afternoon we received a call from area 51 stating they wanted us to fly to a specific coordinate. Upon arrival we were too deploy our security personnel and guard the site. We were instructed that what we were going to see was highly classified and anyone approaching shoot to kill, prior to the security aircraft from area 51 arriving. When we arrived, there was nothing but a smoking hole. When the aircraft from 51 arrived, we were instructed to look for a parachute. We located the parachute with the pilot still attached but was dead. Later we were told that the body was that of the base commander, and that he had taken a 117-stealth fighter for a joyride and was not qualified in the aircraft. The radar tracking showed that the speed at which he had ejected would have killed him instantly and turned his insides too liquid. I guess he knew if he ejected. at least his body would be recovered.

On many occasions Greenpeace would infiltrate the test site, and it is my understanding that each person would receive $1000 each day they were able to stay on the test site undetected. Of course, we knew where they were and would spot them each day and plot their progress. As long as they were not close to a sensitive area, or a detonation location, we would let them continue knowing they were just depleting the funds of Greenpeace.

There was an incident where we had been tracking about 20 people for 10 days, they were heading towards a detonation site. The detonation site was in the mountains and as the underground explosions occurred there was very large boulders on the surface. Detonation was approximately T minus 2 hours, and we flew over them, with loudspeaker, stating if you are in this area leave immediately, an underground detonation is imminent. We flew a pattern that would appear we had not seen them, but we could see them waving their arms and jumping up and down. Obviously, they wanted to depart the area. We had already notified ground vehicles of their location, and they were in route to remove them.

After so many intrusions by Greenpeace, I told the Department of Energy manager for the test site, that I thought I had a plan that would stop Greenpeace personnel from trespassing. He asked if I could explain. I told him, that when we escorted the personnel back to headquarters, that we should be dressed in radiation suits, escort them to the main gate, and suggest they go to the nearest hospital for a checkup. Of course, my idea was rejected.

Preparation for Underground Detonation   *Underground Craters*

In preparation for an underground event, a tremendous amount of equipment had to be installed. The test site resembled the surface of the moon, with all the craters being row, after row. All the craters were depressions where the earth settled moments after an underground detonation.

On another occasion, we were to train with the Task Force 160th and Delta Force for a practice assault on a nuclear site. At the test site that evening Ward Harris was the Duty Pilot and standing by for any alert. I assigned another Pilot for the exercise and Ward was very upset that he was not going to fly the drill. He said that he was a much better choice for the flight as he was a lot better at tactics than the other pilot. I told him I knew this and that was the reason I selected the other pilot and that I was testing our overall preparedness. If he could do the job, then as a unit we were ready. The Pilot did a great job and was given a citation for his actions.

At the test site we worked four days on and four days off in 12-hour shifts. On my four days off I started flying with flight for life at one of the hospitals in Las Vegas. It was a very interesting and challenging assignment. The flight nurses were incredible and more often than not were able to render heroic type Medical aid. On one of the flights, the patient passed away four times and she was able to revive and save the patient. As the pilot we never knew what the mission was for other than medical assistance, to prevent a hero syndrome. I flew for the hospital for two years on my days off while working at the test site.

I also became an FAA Pilot Examiner to issue pilot licenses. This kept me quite busy in my spare time.

After five years at the test site I resigned and took a job in Mexico training pilots in helicopters to support the drug program.

1987 Bell Helicopter Mexico

While working as the Chief Pilot for airborne security at the Nevada Test Site, I received a phone call, in the middle of the night, from the state department asking if I would go to Peru and fly missions for D.E.A., I asked him when it would start and what was the salary. After a discussion I told them I wasn't interested. They asked if I would go to Mexico for a three-month contract and maybe reconsider Peru. After a long conversation I agreed. It was December 1st, so I took a two-week vacation and traveled to Acapulco Mexico to check out the job and see if I wanted to take it. The job was training Mexican FBI pilots in the Bell 212 and 206 helicopters for drug eradication.

Upon arrival the first morning at work I joined five other American flight instructors in the pilot briefing/ready room. We were talking in general when the student pilots all arrived and immediately everyone switched from English to Spanish. I ask one of the instructors what was going on and why everyone was now speaking Spanish. He told me that the students did not speak English, I replied, well, I don't speak Spanish. To his amazement he asked how I got the job, I told him I was asked to join the team of instructors and no one asked me if I spoke Spanish.

Immediately I found myself trying to communicate in a language that I didn't speak. It was difficult to say the least, and mostly communicated through hand signals. As I was learning the language, I began trying to give instruction in Spanish.

In Spanish turn to the left is vida a la izquierda and turn to the right is vida a la derecha. My first attempt was a total failure. As I told the student pilot to turn to the left but pointed to the right. The student obviously was confused and in Spanish ask me to say again.

Again, in Spanish I instructed him to turn to the left, while pointing to the right. He then asked me to be patient and he landed. Looking me in the eye he said holding up his right-hand, APPLE, and then holding up his left hand said, ORANGE. After motioning him to lift to a hover with sign language I then said, "VIDA Ala APPLE," and we turned to the right, so now that I was communicating in Spanish all was well. The personnel and students were great to work with and I really enjoyed the challenge. The Acapulco training center stopped for a two-week Christmas break, so returning back to the US, I resigned from my job and prepared for the job in Mexico. All of my co-workers and friends thought I was crazy to resign a great paying job and go to Mexico for a 90-day contract. When asked what I would do after the 90 days were up, I told them I had never been on an around the world cruise and would address that problem when it arose.

After 3 months, I was promoted to assistant general manager, and transferred to headquarters in Mexico City. This job was both challenging and gratifying to say the least. It was like being a standardization pilot while traveling around the country. I would go to each base, give training, and check-rides.

I received news that my first student, from Acapulco was killed while flying a mission for DEA along with two DEA agents and a Mexican General. They were flying to verify that a poppy field had been sprayed in the mountains. While flying up the Canyon to inspect the field, the drug cartel pulled cables across the valley and on their return, they hit the cables and crashed.

After three years working with the Mexican authorities, I was asked to leave the country. This was because, Bell Helicopters was notified that a large operation on the Mexican border with Texas was approaching and they needed six more Bell 212 pilots trained and certified. I hired six additional instructor pilot's and assigned them to the Acapulco training center to await their student's arrival.

John Cronin was the general manager in Mexico for Bell Helicopters, but was in Fort Worth Texas, at Corporate Headquarters. With John gone this left me in charge as acting general manager and I would take the hit. I am really very happy that John was not there at the time and that I would be held responsible. Mr. Cronin was a great boss to work with and an asset for the company.

In a final mission briefing meeting with DEA, U.S. Embassy staff, US Senators, and US Congressman, the Mexican director was telling the members in attendance what a great job Bell Helicopters had done in preparation for the mission. He stated in fact they have done such an outstanding job, that three of the students had graduated two weeks early. The gentleman setting on my right was from the US Embassy and was writing everything down. I asked what he was doing, and he stated he was preparing a memo to send back to Washington.

I advised him not to mail the letter because nothing the director had said was truthful. He was very puzzled and asked, what do you mean. I told him not one of the six students had ever arrived in Acapulco for their training. When the meeting completed, he went to the director's office and asked why he had spoken untruthful. The director replied what do you mean? I've heard none of the students ever arrived for training. The director said, well that is true, but who told you this. When he was told that I had informed him, he asked that Bell helicopter be given a message. The message was, Bell

Helicopter's contract is up for renewal next week and if Ray is still in Mexico, they will not be awarded the contract.

An executive vice president, a vice president of bell helicopters and Mr. Cronin came to my apartment and told me the Mexican government wanted me out of Mexico by the end of next week. They told the Mexican Authorities, no way, Ray has four to six weeks to leave Mexico and was going to Acapulco for a well-deserved vacation. Well this left Bell no alternative but to transfer me out of Mexico.

The company wanted me to return to Fort Worth at the main training center and work there, but I told them it did not pay enough, and I could not do it. They said they would like me to go to Manama Bahrain and work for Bell Arabia a division of Bell for a year and then they were opening a new operation in Europe and wanted me to be the general manager. I accepted the job in Manama and trained the Bahraini Air Force helicopter squadron. While there I trained and certified all their pilots for their instrument rating. After one year to the day I resigned from bell Arabia.

Looking for other employment I contacted gulf airlines and during the interview they asked if I could leave in three days for France and be trained on the Boeing 737 airliner. As we were discussing my hiring one of the pilots walked into the room and said boss, we have a problem. Doha Qatar has just announced that all of our helicopter pilots there had to be instrument certified. Hearing this, I asked how much that job would pay. To my surprise, Starting pay for the helicopter instrument instructor was the same as a mid-life 737 copilot. As this was my last day of employment with Bell Arabia, I accepted the job in Doha Qatar and left Bahrain.

January 17th, 1971 Gulf War

$\mathfrak{f}$or five years I flew offshore to the oil and gas fields off Doha Qatar, carrying personnel and supplies to the platforms. In the Middle East during Ramadan the Arabs were not able to eat or drink during the day and out of respect, the pilots would abstain. Normally I would radio ahead to the platform and place an order for food and drink. When flying the Arabs to the platforms during Ramadan, the passengers would insist that I order food to keep my blood sugar up. So, we would order, and eat and drink in front of them.

While working for Gulf Helicopters, every six months we had one month off. My month off was just beginning and we left for home in Las Vegas. The flight itself lasted some 28 hours. Upon arrival, we were with my mom and dad and of course jet lagged to the Max. Everyone was asleep except for me, it was 3:00 AM and I was watching CNN news when Operation Desert Shield began. I knew if we were to return to Doha, we had to leave immediately. For one-year mom and dad had planned to return with us to Doha for vacation. I woke everyone and advised of the update to the Iraqi war. I informed mom and dad that if they still wanted to go, we had to leave on the next flight. Mom was concerned as to the safety of the trip. I told her if I was concerned at all, I would not let Pam (my wife) go with me. Mom understood, agreed, everyone packed, and we caught the first flight out of Las Vegas to Doha that morning. The flight took over 50 hours door to door. The flight path circumnavigated Qatar flew over Russia and approached from the South landing in Muscat Oman. There was a 10-hour layover, and we slept in the first-class lounge. Finally arriving in Doha jet lagged to the max, everyone slept the remainder of the day.

Mom and Dad were very excited, because this was their first trip overseas. Pam and I were on the US Ambassadors short list of invitees as host at his functions. My mother could not believe she was going to a party at the US Ambassador's residence. When the war was over, at one of the parties for General Schwarzkopf, she could not believe it when he hugged her and said thank you for your support.

The British expats in Doha were very concerned about the scud missiles being launched towards Qatar and had requested gas mask from their embassy. A few of the US expats had also requested the ambassador distribute mask for them. The ambassador tried to reason with them by explaining there was no danger. He finally distributed mask to all US expats. Understandably my brothers were concerned that I had taken their mother and father to a war zone. Although we were very safe, I decided to make a phony video.

The video started with a statement by me asking, is that a siren I hear. I then told everyone to put on their gas mask. I didn't know it, but mom was claustrophobic and did not enjoy the mask at all. Anyway, I sent the video to my brothers. To this day, they have not mentioned it to me, so I don't know how it was perceived. About six weeks later, mom and dad returned home and had

Mom. Dad & Me

enjoyed their trip to Doha. I was glad they had come, for now they knew we were safe and didn't have to worry.

As far as flying during the Gulf War, sometimes it was challenging. It was like synchronized jump rope, first military aircraft would take off for Baghdad, then I would take off for the oil field.

Pam became the ambassador's liaison for the US Embassy to the military. We agreed to host 20 servicemen each night for pizza and beer. We did this every day until the war was over. In Qatar expats were only allowed a small amount of liquor on a ration card. The ambassador new what we were doing and issued us a special ration card.

After Desert Shield completed, the night before Desert Storm began, we had the F16 squadron pilots over for beer and pizza. I'm sure they all knew the war was about to begin as they were very quiet. One of them asked me, what is it like in combat. I've never flown in combat but have been shot at many times in the past. I ask if they had ever played football and if so, remember at the beginning of the game you could not remember any of the plays until you were hit for the first time and then it all came back. I told him not to worry because all of your training kicks in, and everything will be fine. The next day on the Evening News was one of the pilots we had hosted that night, and he was the first pilot shot down and taken as a POW. The picture that was shown on TV indicated that he had been beaten, however later we found out that the bruising was from when he ejected.

Setting at home in our villa one evening we heard a dull thud. What we had heard was a scud missile impact about 3 miles to the north. There was a very shallow crater because the fuel required for the missile to travel this distance left little room for explosives. DOD after inspection presented Pam and I with a piece of the scud enclosed in plastic.

General Schwarzkopf was a very humble man, and a pleasure to meet. When I told him how grateful I was of his leadership and tried to thank him, he stopped me and said, no it is my pleasure to meet you, and thank you for all the support you have given to my men.

It truly was a pleasure to welcome all of the men and women into our home each night. We developed many friendships and it left a large void in our lives when the war was over, and they left.

1992 50th Birthday

September 28th, 1992

On my 50th birthday I was in Doha Qatar. That day the pilots asked if I could stay late and do the drying runs because they had to leave, so I stayed for an extra 2 hours after work starting up 12 helicopters drying the engines. When I finished, Larry, one of the other pilot's said, let's go to my house and have a drink before you go home, I agreed and called my wife, she said the women are over today for the American women's association meeting so maybe you could go to Larry's house so we did. OK, unknown to me all the mechanics had got together and made a casket lined with silk and had painted it black with a golden cross saying RIP on the top. When we left Larry's to walk down to my Villa, looking towards my front porch and wondering what the Hell's on my porch. As I got closer it was obvious that it was a coffin. When I opened the door there was over 100 people dressed in black and white with arm band's saying rest in peace. A good friend of mine was the manager of the Doha Sheraton Hotel and had offered to cater the party with all the booze, food, and staff, really nice of him, thank you Gerhart.

As everybody left, we were downstairs sitting in the living room maybe five or six of us and I kept hearing a bam, clank, bam, coming from upstairs. Wondering what the heck, I went upstairs, and the master bathroom was on fire. It was tile falling off the wall that I could hear, so I'm getting water out of the sink with my hands throwing it on the fire. I yelled fire and other guys came up and started pouring water until we put the fire out. The fire had started with a cigarette that was not out, dumped from an ashtray, into a trash container under the sink.

All of the staff from the Sheraton that had been serving food said, don't worry Boss we will clean it up. We went back downstairs had a few more drinks while they cleaned upstairs blah blah blah blah blah. Anyway, that was my 50th birthday. Another memorable moment in time.

1993 Doha Qatar

lying in Doha Qatar was great, but I needed something else to do. The Doha Players Theatre was something I became interested in. One evening while driving by I stopped too check it out. I was told there were additions for an upcoming play the following Wednesday, so I decided to check it out and possibly audition.

On the evening of auditions while setting in the audience they ask if I could read from a script. I told them sure and started reading. However, as I was reading it became apparent that the script, was for a woman. I informed them of my discovery, and they replied, that's Okay just please keep reading. Upon conclusion of auditions I was informed that I had the leading role in the play. However, the part was for a woman. This play was referred to as a pantomime. The pantomime is very popular in Britain where the leading woman is played by a man and the leading man is played by a woman. This play was Jack and the Beanstalk. I have never had so much fun while performing in this play. When you wear a wig, earrings, and high heel shoes, you can't help but laugh at yourself.

As an American I believed that pantomime was really a mime. If pantomime was brought to the United states and performed, I believe it would be very successful.

Pantomime is performed every year in Europe at Christmas and always a fairy tale.

I received a phone call stating that the present chairwoman was going to put the theater into bankruptcy and asked if I would run for chairman. Later I was elected as chairman of the theater and was the first none British to hold this position. I managed the theater by committee, and it was very successful.

Each year the theater performed six major plays along with a few 1 act plays. I can remember as chairman being put on the spot one evening when the star of a play went down sick. I received a phone call at 2 PM the afternoon of opening night and was told that I would have to take his place. The personnel on my staff were all very talented and resourceful. They told me not to worry that they would meet me at the theater in 30 minutes to help prepare. They took the entire script, photocopied and reduced it to appear as a small notebook. The play was called, The Inspector Calls. Luckily it was a one act play but serious in nature. Normally for a one act play like this there would be a very small crowd in attendance.

As the word traveled throughout Doha's expat community that I would be doing what they thought was impossible and stepping in to play the main character at the last moment with only a few hours' notice, the theater with 380 seats was sold out by opening curtain. I'm sure they all wanted to see me stammer and make a fool of myself.

I remember trying to follow the script from my small notebook when all of a sudden, they lost me by jumping four or five pages ahead in the script. The actor's line had asked me a question that was a yes or no answer. I could not locate in the script where he had jumped so I couldn't answer, the actor ask me the question again an I looked at him and said *"As soon as I find where you are in the script I'll be glad to answer."* That one line brought the house down with laughter.

In my childhood there was a play called "Dawn Boy" that I starred in, and I've always wanted to be back on stage.

At one of my committee meetings I was informed the director for the Sound of Music had to leave for London for emergency surgery and we had no major play for the slot. Auditions were well underway, and the director was planning to continue with the play upon her return. In order for the tradition of, The Show Must Go On, my production manager stated she had the script, and music score for the play "The King And I". However, she did not have anyone to play the king or to direct it. She said the only way the committee figured we would be able to fill the slot at such a late moment, was if I played the king and directed the play. I told them they were all crazy. Well they weren't as crazy as I thought, and I started holding auditions 4 days later. With a lot of teamwork, the play was very successful.

I was in several plays and directed a few. The Doha Theater was a great experience for me while in Qatar and made the time pass by very fast. Although it was very enjoyable, it was a lot of work. Thank you, Doha Players!

While flying For Gulf Helicopters, a division of Gulf Airlines, I was the training officer for all pilot staff, and a line captain. This was a great job and I enjoyed it very much.

One day on a flight to the Northfield gas production platform 80 miles out, I had dropped off 12 passengers and picked up 6 for return to Doha Qatar. Approximately 25 minutes into the return flight I received a radio call asking me to return to the platform as there were VIPs to board the helicopter. I advised them I was unable to return because I did not have the fuel. Approximately 5 more minutes elapsed and again, I was asked to return to pick up the VIP's. Again, I informed them I did not have enough fuel to return. Another 10 minutes passed, and the chief pilot radioed that I had been requested to return to the Northfield for additional passengers. I told him I was

15 minutes from Doha, please advise. He then stated he thought I was just lifting off from the platform and said to disregard.

After securing the helicopter, I went to the chief pilot's office and ask if he wanted me to make a written report, he stated that it wouldn't be necessary, and he would give the general manager a heads up. The following day the chief pilot called me into his office and told me he had to let me go. I asked, go where. He then informed me that the oil company had notified Gulf Helicopters and told them I was not acceptable as a pilot for their contract. The reason they gave was that they did not pay for pilots to make the decision as to what passengers they would pick up. I told the chief I was going to speak with the general manager. When I arrived in his office, he immediately stated that he knew he had cost me my job. When asked what he meant, he said he told the customer that he was sure if I had known they were VIP's I would have returned and pick them up. He also stated that if I contacted or anyone contacted the customer on my behalf, that I would not receive my $25,000 severance pay. I forgot to mention that the general manager was British, and a very weak person at best. He was right I'm sure, if I had told the customer what really happened, politics as a major contributor, he would have been fired.

Everyone in the company was shocked that I had been terminated and prepared a going away party. As the word got out to the expat community, there was a large turnout and the party was well received by my wife and myself.

In life sometimes things happen that are beyond our control. Although my wife and I we're not ready to leave Doha, we accepted the challenge and left for Las Vegas Nevada.

1995 Point Barrow Alaska

fter leaving Doha Qatar in the Middle East, ariving in Las Vegas I flew Grand Canyon Scenic tours by helicopter for one year. This experience alone was very gratifying to say the least. The flights were approximately two hours duration. After the year was up, I was offered a job and point Barrow Alaska as a rescue pilot.

I went to Point Barrow. It was a dramatic change in climate, going from plus 130F to minus 50F. When my wife arrived, it was just after a snow melt, and everything was covered in mud. She took one look outside the airplane door and did not want to get off. However, it didn't take her very long to adjust to the new climate and culture. I had been in Barrow for about 1 month and had an apartment set up and ready for her arrival.

Prior to me arriving, the company sent me too Wichita Kansas for Cessna Caravan school. After arrival in Point Barrow, I was sent to Dallas Fort Worth for the Bell 214 ST school. When the schools were completed, I was ready to work. The following year they sent me to Tucson Arizona for Lear Jet 31A school.

I was hired as a line pilot, and soon after arrival was promoted to chief training captain. The weather was different from anything I had ever flown in my career. I remember the first mission that I flew as copilot after my initial arrival was the most frightening experience I've ever had. That evening, the chief pilot called me and said we have a flight. Looking outside the weather was so bad I was sure this was just a test to see if I would go. The wind was blowing 45 knots and overcast at 250 feet. We entered the helicopter, doors opened and we were pulled out by a tug. The chief as pilot in command started both engines. I remember thinking he is really taking this to the limit for this test. To my surprise, he pulled pitch and we took off. The mission was to locate a person that was six hours overdue on his snow machine. We could only fly 40 knots of air speed and 50 feet above the snow-covered tundra. After numerous course changes while following a snow machine trail, and two hours of searching, we located the missing person. When we arrived back at base, the captain stated, Ray you can go on inside while I shut down and secure the helicopter. I left and went to my office, started packing all of my personal items and waiting on the captain. When he arrived, he asked, what are you doing. I apologized to him stating I just thought I was a pilot and I could not hold a candle to him. He asked, what do you mean. I told him the weather was well beyond my experience level. He told me the weather was pretty bad, but I didn't have to fly in weather like this if I wasn't comfortable. I told him my stomach was in my throat the entire flight, and I was scared to death. His reply shocked me. He stated that he felt very comfortable knowing that a man like me with my experience was there to back him up. For the 5 years I was in Alaska, the captain could not fly a mission alone as he had no confidence in himself, but if there was anyone in the copilot seat, he was fine.

The skill level of all the helicopter pilots, with regards to bad weather was well below average and as the new chief training captain, it was my job to correct this. I asked a few of the pilots how they survived flying in the bad weather, they replied, oh we didn't fly until the weather was good. We waited while playing spades or hearts. The company's mission was search and rescue, but they treated it like anything but the mission. At Point Barrow during the winter there are three months of total darkness. Flying in the weather that is normal on the north slope is extremely dangerous all the time, especially in the dark. I was able to introduce, train, and certify all of the pilots with Night Vision Goggles. With this asset it increased the safety of flight astronomically.

On arrival in Point Barrow, there were 8 pilots to man the duty roster 24 hours 7 days per week for two aircraft. Each pilot was averaging 500 flight hours per year. I was instrumental in obtaining personal locating beacons (PLBs) for anyone leaving the villages. This alone reduced the flying hours of each pilot to 225 per year. These beacons limited the search time by giving an exact location for the rescue. After six months on the job I was promoted to chief pilot. At this point I increased the training of all pilot staff and helped then to maintain a high level of preparedness and proficiency.

Early one morning I received a radio call that a 55 mile stretch of the ice along the shoreline had broken off and was drifting out to sea. At the time the whaling season was well underway and there were six whaling camps out on the ice. There were approximately 350 natives that were retrieving captured whales and manning the whaling camps. I remember the weather was heavy fog and the wind was calm. Driving to the airport I had to have the door open looking at the road. I sat in the helicopter engines running for about 30 minutes before there was a break in the fog and I was able to take off. I was told that I flew over one of the whaling camps at about 150 feet and they could not see me, nor I see them. Each whaling camp was able to give me a latitude / longitude position, thus making it easier to locate them. The fog was moving around and opening periodically. With each break in the fog I was able to recover personnel from the ice. After getting all of the people off the ice and back in Barrow, I was able to go home and get some rest after 12 hours of flying.

The Director of Search and Rescue called me on the radio and said the natives wanted their snow machines, boats and equipment removed from the ice and brought back to Barrow. I told him it would be cheaper to buy them new ones than to fly the Helicopter. He reminded me that they owned the helicopter and wanted their equipment back. I left home and once again started flying. I would lift 4-5 snow machines at a time and fly them back to the shore. They would load the boats with their supplies and personal gear for transport. My co-pilot was very low time pilot, so I had to do all the lifting. My crew chief would always leave a PLB beacon on the ice pan, so we could return until all equipment was removed from each whaling camp. It took nine days two complete the removal of all equipment from the ice while flying 10 hours and sleeping for 8. Surprisingly when lifting the last sling load from the ice the GPS location showed that we had drifted 55 miles out to sea.

For several months after this incident each time I would be shopping at the grocery store, or just walking along a street, elders from the village would approach me, shake my hand, and say thank you. It wasn't registering with me as to why they were doing this. I guess three or four months had passed when I was summoned to the high school auditorium by the director. The annual whaling conference was underway, and he wanted me there because they had a presentation for me. Still I did not understand why. I asked the director why they are doing this. He said to me, you really don't know do you. He then explained to me that some 60 years prior a similar situation had occurred and that an entire village of 180 people had drifted to sea on the ice and were never seen again. All of this time the people of Barrow were thanking me for saving their brothers, sisters, mother and father's. It was quite humbling for me once I understood. I had only looked at this rescue as doing my job.

I had a call one afternoon Advising me that an elder was overdue on a trip he was taking on his snow machine to his cabin 14 miles to the South, he never arrived. The search for this gentleman was an all-out effort lasting five days. We found him on the 5th afternoon 114 miles east of his cabin. When we landed beside him, the flight nurse was approaching him, and the gentleman stated holding out his left arm and pointing with this right hand, 'I NEED IV'.

The north slope men were some of the strongest on the planet. At 70 years of age they would think nothing of leaving the village on a snow machine for 1-2 weeks pulling a sleigh with 100 gallons of gas, going Caribou hunting.

My wife started working for a local charter company as a flight dispatcher. They would haul freight and passengers to all the villages. She really enjoyed her work and seemed very happy working with aviation. She was a private airplane pilot and understood the day to day flying requirements. One morning she called me at work very shook up and said that they had a crash and the pilot was killed. She had a hard time getting over this and didn't want to go back to work. After a few days she appeared to be a lot better and returned to her job.

A few months later, early one morning, I received a call from search and rescue's office advising me that a plane had just crashed into the ocean off the end of the runway. When I arrived, we discovered there were eight fatalities, and it was one of her planes. When I told her, she was never the same and quit her job and never went back to work. The pilot was a close friend and manager of their base operations.

Two years later I hired a pilot that had flown with me all over the world. His name is Ward Harris. When Ward arrived, one evening I called and told him we had a flight. At the time the weather was blowing snow, 250 feet overcast and 35 knots of wind. Like me, Ward thought this was a test and went along with it. We took off destination Wainwright Alaska, 85 miles to the South West. I flew down the shoreline and as we were getting closer to Wainwright the weather was deteriorating. On final approach to Wainwright I could see the glow of a runway light and hovered from light to light. The patient was a lady that was having a difficult birth and without a hospital both her and the baby would not survive. For all flight crews, it is imperative that they not know the reason for the flight to prevent hero actions. Sometimes people die and then the mission becomes just a recovery.

When we arrived back at point Barrow, I told Ward he could go on up to the office and I would shut down the aircraft. To my surprise when I arrived upstairs there was Ward packing his personal items, just as I had done. I ask ward what he was doing, he said boss, I can't do this I was scared to death. I started laughing and he said why are you laughing. I told him I've had the same experience that you just went through, trust me Ward, you're going to love it up here. Two years later I finished a five-year contract and was leaving. Ward took my place and continued as the main Helicopter rescue pilot.

The North Slope Bourgh Search and Rescue (SAR) was truly a search and rescue operation. The Helicopter would locate, package and transport the injured to the nearest village airport where they would transfer the patient to their Lear Jet if necessary, and transport to Anchorage Hospital. The Lear Jet would on average make 4-5 trips to Anchorage every week. Flying for The SAR was the most gratifying job I have ever had.

By the way, the BELL 214-ST Helicopter is the number one helicopter for this job and when I left the North Slope Bourgh Search and Rescue, I truly missed flying it.

1999 Aviation Specialties

I had left Alaska to help a friend in Boise Idaho. He was trying to bring night vision goggles into the civilian world. Both of us had been flying for the US government Department of Energy for five years and had brought civilian flying with night vision goggles into existence. He told me he needed help and ask if I would come. Mike Atwood and I had been friends for about 9 years. When I arrived, we agreed that Mike would obtain the contracts, and I would train and certify the pilots, along with flight crew. Mike named the company Aviation Specialties Unlimited (ASU). We struggled for the first two years trying to get the Federal Aviation Administration, (FAA) to approve our program. No one in the FAA was familiar with night vision which made our job incredibly difficult. Mike had sold 7 or 8 contracts to various hospital medevac crews, and they had goggles locked up in secure cabinets. The common response from the different FAA agencies was, night vision goggles are dangerous. Each time I heard this response I would ask, have you ever flown night vision. They always responded, no but a friend of mine told me they would shut down in a lighted area and were dangerous.

During this delay of approval from the FAA, there were several fatal medevac crashes at night, when at the time of the crash they had night vision goggles locked up and waiting for their training to be approved by the FAA. Finally, through much frustration I told the FAA that the next medevac crash that occurred at night without night vision that I would contact all media and hold a news conference describing how they were killing people because of ignorance. Wow, this generated a very positive response. The FAA sent a representative from the Rotorcraft Directive office in Fort Worth Texas to check out our training program. With the usual unorganized, and unqualified personnel assignments, they sent a female inspector that had only flown night vision on a 10 minutes demo flight. On her arrival, she said she was there to certify our company for two pilot night vision goggle training. I told her, negative our program is for single pilot take off to landing night vision goggle operations. She corrected me by saying, no this is for two pilot certifications.

This conversation was taking place at night in our hangar. I told her, if I understand you correctly, looking out the window into the darkness, I could legally take off single pilot to the east without night vision, fly into the mountain and kill myself, however I cannot put on NVG's, see the mountain and fly around it, is this correct. She gave no response at this time, and Mike instructed me to go and have a cup of coffee. She left without ever flying with us and returned to her office. Later that week I received a phone call from a gentleman that was from the same office that she was. He said that he would be coming to inspect our operation. On his arrival I gave him a full 8-hour ground school for NVG's, and then took him on a one-hour flight. I took him into the mountains, flew around for a while and returned back to the airport. He could not believe how much the goggles had improved the safety of our night flight. After the flight he said the reason the FAA had always denied our request for so long was because they thought we were teaching a military maneuver called nap of the earth flying. This was based solely on one of the classes called terrain interpretation. The name Terrain Interpretation was one of the courses the FAA had said must be taught, and it had nothing to do with the maneuver called nap-of-the-earth. They were dealing with the good old boy syndrome by not approving our course until another company, (I will not mention) completed their course and submitted for approval. The course they submitted was our course almost word for word, and they received the first approved Night Vision Training course. Finally, we received certification and our training program was authorized. Within the next 12 months, after a two-year delay, we trained and certified nine hospital medevac flight programs to fly single pilot, takeoff to landing with night vision goggles.

Mike and I were invited to FAA headquarters in Washington DC to assist in writing the regulations governing night vision goggle flight. We had finished the drafted proposal, and it was in the system for approval. Shortly after submission, it was delayed, and was put on the back burner because of 911.

This did not slow us down with the training, and certification process. Our clients expanded to include, various police departments, sheriff department's, and foreign military. In the next few years we had trained and certified 37 hospital programs, 22 law enforcement agencies, and 4 foreign military programs. It was very Gratifying seeing all of the programs starting to fly with night vision, and of course the safety of all was improved by several 100%.

Mike and I started the night vision program for the Nevada Test Site, INEL in Idaho, Savana River, and Hanford Washington. These sites were all Atomic testing sites and protected by helicopters and an airborne security force. When the NVG's were added to the missions the safety and performance increased by 200%.

The company had to expand its services to include cockpit lighting modifications. The Process was a challenging one because each different model / type had to be inspected, approved, and issued a type certificate from the FAA. The same problems surfaced with the FAA that we had had in the past certifying our training program. This brought on a whole new headache dealing with the FAA.

ASU is the leader in Night Vision Cockpit Modification, Sales, and Training. The company is known worldwide and respected by the aviation industry.

I had been with Mike developing the company for nine years, and finally reached burnout dealing with the FAA bureaucracy. I resigned and accepted a job flying a 20 passenger Bell 214 ST helicopter with night vision, in support of the US military in the Philippines fighting Al-Qaeda.

2009
Zamboanga
Philippines

Evergreen Helicopters had the contract supporting the US military both with helicopters and fixed-wing aircraft in Zamboanga Philippines. I had traveled there Several times to give training and type rides for pilots and a Bell Helicopter 214 ST. They finally offered me a position as line pilot and trainer, and I accepted.

When arriving in Zamboanga I was quite surprised to see the same Bell 214 ST's that I had flown for the North Slope Borough in Point Barrow Alaska. As I've stated earlier, this helicopter is truly a pleasure to fly. The job was supporting forward bases with supplies and moving troops. The job offers many challenges as we are up against al Qaeda. Each morning prior to departure, we received a security, and intelligence briefing. We are covering the island of Mindanao, Bacilan, Cebu, Cagayan De Oro, and the island of Tawi Tawi. These areas were filled with Al Qaeda and dangerous to fly in. They were famous for flying very large kites up into the clouds out of sight, with clear monofilament fishing line. On many occasions upon landing, I would find fishing line wrapped around the flight controls and we had to remove it before taking off. On one flight, while on final approach to a confined area on a mountain Ridge, as I started to land, I noticed that my tail rotor control pedals were jammed. As the helicopter started to spin, I was able to dive the helicopter off of the cliff gaining airspeed and land safely back at the airport. The fishing line was melted around the control rods and we had to use a hacksaw to remove it.

Tail Rotor Pedals Locked with Fishing Line

My aircraft only received bullet holes on one flight. One Military passenger received a bullet wound in his right leg. We were losing fuel but had enough to return to our main base. Especially on day flights they were always shooting at us but never scored a hit. There was one landing area on the island just South of Zamboanga that the gunfire was very heavy. We started flying there only at night-time with night vision and the shooting stopped. Each flight to this location was always at a different time each night.

Our flight schedule was such that we had a lot of free time and this is when I took up the game of golf. EAAB Golf course was on the Filipino Air Force Base in conjunction with the International Airport. The driving range for the golf course was just outside of our living area front gate. I started playing 18 holes seven days a week. Playing golf there at EAAB was quite different than any other place I had played. For a foursome teeing off, there would be 16 people leaving the tee-box. Each player would have, an umbrella girl, caddy, and a ball-boy. This made playing in the hot sun a lot easier.

Each year at Christmas I sponsored a tournament for the caddy's and would team them with an American. With the help of some volunteers, I obtained sponsors for prizes for the winners. Also, through collections from fellow employees and military personnel we were able to support a local orphan home with clothes, and gifts for the children. It was an unbelievable feeling seeing the children's eyes light up when Santa walked into the room and gave them all a gift. I was told later that they had never seen Santa before. Rose and I still send clothes and toy's each year to the orphanage. In addition, we would have a 10,000 peso ($213.00) first prize for the winning caddy, of course the American would receive a small trophy.

My caddie and I would always tee off first so that when we finished, we could arrange food for all of the players, and of course not eligible to win. I would send him to Jollibee (a Philippine hamburger place) for 100 hamburgers. As the players finished, they would receive a hamburger and wait for the others to finish. On the second annual tournament, after all players completed playing, while talking to my caddie in preparation for the awards ceremony, I looked up and saw an umbrella girl standing off to the side with no hamburger. I told my caddie to ask her if she had received one. She replied no, so my first words to Rosalinda (my future wife) was, hamburger little girl. I had hired 2-3 other umbrella girls in the past and always had a sunburn and now didn't have a regular one. About two weeks had past when again I looked up and saw Rosalinda for the second time. I asked her if she was working and available as I was about to tee off. She replied yes and away we went. Upon completion of the 18 holes, I was impressed with her service, I told her that I played every day, and asked if she would consider being my full-time umbrella girl. She agreed, and that was the end of my sun burns. I had the only golf cart at the golf course and while driving, during a conversation she told me she had just graduated from college. I asked why she was working as an umbrella girl, and she said that she made a lot more money and had always wanted to learn the game but couldn't afford it. The golf club allowed her to play for free every Monday. I asked if she wanted to play along with me and that I would pay the fees. She agreed, and after my first six-week tour in the Philippines playing with her, I spoke with my wife in Boise, and told her of the young girl, and I wanted to buy her a cheap set of clubs. My wife agreed, and so it was. I presented the clubs to Rosalinda upon my return and could not believe how fast she was learning the game. After my next six-week rotation, I bought her a set of Hy-bred clubs and she started beating everyone at the club. The club management became very jealous and told me she could not play anymore because she was not a member. This did not set well with me, so I paid for her club membership. A lifetime membership for a Philippine citizen was only $100.00. As the players began to notice her ability, the group called the gamblers, asked her to join them each day for a game. This group consisted of, lawyers, doctors, generals, and a judge. I always had Rosalinda playing from the men's tee box, and this group insisted she play from the women's tee. Each day she would win their money, finally one of the attorney's demanded that she plays from the men's tee. The Judge looked at him and said, are you kidding, she is a woman and will play from the women's tee. Rose made a hole in one on a short par four and now everyone knew who she was.

While still working in the Philippines, I was contacted by McDermott helicopters in Australia to provide ground training, flight training, and certification on a Bell 214 ST helicopter for 7 pilots. On my way to the Philippines for a six-week tour, I routed through Australia. McDermott had several Bell 214-single engine helicopters that these pilots were flying, and this made their initial training easier. This was my first trip to Australia, and it was very enjoyable. I have made two trips to Australia for pilot training and certification in the 214 ST's and looking forward to the next trip. This trip enabled me to purchase a newer golf cart for Zamboanga.

Pam, my wife, became very ill and passed away. It was a life changer for me, and I will miss her forever. About 18 months after my wife passed, I asked Rosalinda to marry me and move to America. At first, she was very hesitant but finally agreed. Asking Rosalinda to marry me was not an easy decision for me, as there is a 40-year difference in our age. Each time I would tell Rose that I was too old to remarry, she would reply age is only what you feel in your heart. Needless to say, she enabled me to accept the age difference and get married.

I sold my golf cart, packed up and we left for the states. We were married in Las Vegas, at the Little Church of the West, and played golf the next morning with my best man at the Las Vegas Country Club. We returned to my home in Boise ID and stayed there for one week, locked the house up and accepted a job with AAR in Melbourne Florida, we drove to Melbourne, and rented an apartment on a golf course. This worked out great, because Rose could play golf while I was at the office / or traveling. The company told me I could still live in Idaho, and just travel as needed. We sold our home in Boise Idaho, and Rose and I bought a new house in Meridian Idaho, on the outskirts of Boise. One year later the company wanted me to move permanently back to Melbourne. We sold the house and moved to Melbourne, Florida. Now 10 years later, Rose and I along with our three teenage kids are still in Melbourne, and all are playing golf. All of the kids are on the High School golf teams and doing very well. They are Hoping for a college scholarship. My youngest daughter Brittany told me when she Became a Professional Golfer she would build Rose and I a two-story house. I told her I didn't want a two-story house, and she replied, Dad it will have an elevator.

2012 AAR
Melbourne, FL

After leaving the Philippines, I started working for AAR Corporation. My Position was Senior Training Captain for the helicopter fleet. The company had a 214 ST that I had flown in Australia, and it was very nice to continue flying the ST. The company trained me for the Sikorsky S-61, and the Puma 330J. These are also large helicopters and enjoyable to fly.

My first mission in the S-61 was to ferry one from Melbourne to Montana. The trip was Ok, but I didn't like the helicopter. The second mission was to ferry another one from Vancouver Canada back to Melbourne. The company assigned a new hire pilot straight from the Navy as my co-pilot, so I was training him all the way back. As we were flying over the Rocky Mountain range, he stated that he had never flown in the mountains. This was not the only surprise I had on this flight. This time I really liked the S-61 and found out later it was because the company we bought it from knew how to rig the helicopter. I would train pilots at the home base, and travel to France each month to train our pilots in a level D full motion flight simulator.

I was the chief Instructor for the companies VERT REP (Vertical Reference) contract. I went to sea on a US Navy Freighter flying a Puma 330J helicopter re-supplying the US Navy fleet for 60 days. The company lost the contract, and this was the last trip at sea for AAR. We supported The US Navy off the coast of Africa and the middle east. There were two carrier groups we re-supplied.

When I was in the Navy onboard the aircraft carrier USS Hornet CVS-12, the helicopters the Navy was using was the S-61. Although, I had been told that I should seek employment with the Acme Truck Driving School by my 1st flight instructor, here I was re-supplying the carrier's by helicopter. I really enjoyed flying on VERT REP and the time at sea seemed to pass fairly quick. The flying was with two pilots and both were needed to perform the mission.

Re-Supplying a Carrier in the Middle East

I would travel to Marseilles France every month to train the VERT REP pilots to maintain their instrument currency. I do not care for France; however, Marseille is quite nice, the locals are friendly, and Americans are liked. I dealt with several French people when I was in Doha Qatar and did not enjoy their company due to their personalities by letting everyone know they were better than you. I was told by several of the pilots that in the South of France the people are more friendly, and I found this to be very true.

The company would send me to the island of Guam two to three times a year to give instrument currency check-rides in one of our Puma 330 J's. I enjoyed the island of Guam and my wife traveled with me to Guam a few times. Upon completion, we would then fly on to the Philippines to visit her family.

Back in Melbourne, I was doing pilot initial new hire training in the PUMA 330 J and another training captain was doing maintenance flights on one of the S 61's. We both were flying in the same area on and off for approximately 2 hours. We were supposed to trade our students for training because the student he had in the S-61 was just an acting copilot for reading the checklist and waiting to be checked out in the Puma. We agreed not to trade because he had one more test to complete and thought it would be best if he used the same copilot. With that understanding, I secured my aircraft and left for home. As I pulled into my driveway 20 minutes later, I was informed the other aircraft had crashed and both crew we're dead. The death of the flight crew was hard for me to handle, maybe because I had just spoke with them 20-30 minutes prior. 12:03 PMhe Captain was a close friend and will be missed.

The company closed the air division of AAR after being awarded a NATO contract. I left AAR and started full time with Archangel Aviation in Melbourne, Florida as Chief Pilot.

ARCHANGEL 2019

$f$or the past five years I have been working part time for Archangel, and now have joined full time as chief pilot. The working conditions and atmosphere are unbelievably smooth, happy and very gratifying. We are flying a Sikorski S-76C+, Bell 412, Bell 206 helicopters, Cessna Sky Masters and CASA 212 airplanes. When I first joined Archangel, the company was providing a platform for skydivers, and still provides this service. It has evolved now providing security for all Space X launches and recoveries. Archangel patrols a clear zone offshore for each launch from Cape Canaveral for SpaceX. This service is provided for both day and night launches. The farthest distance offshore for clearance protection was 25 nautical miles. We are responsible to verify that this area remains clear of all boats and personnel prior to launch. Recently SpaceX has started sending astronauts back into space in support of the space station. We of course provide the security for launch and also for the capsule recovery. During Capsule recoveries, we are 50 miles offshore of the Florida coast either East side or West side. It is incredible to witness the launch from about 1 mile from the pad especially, when they recover both rockets simultaneously back next to the Launchpad. William Shatner was just launched into space and I am so happy for him. After the Star Trek tv series, I'm sure it was a life-changing experience for him.

While Working for Archangel I was contacted by Pelican flight school to see if I would be interested in a part time position with their company as chief flight instructor both for helicopter and airplane. I met with the owner and manager and decided to accept the position. We have a very successful Flight School and all of the Staff are very professional. We have a very high first pass record due to the quality of instruction given by all of our Instructors. Pelican offers both fixed-wing and helicopter training.

Anna Stepanova as manager of the school, does an incredible job herding 150 students and sometimes I believe she has to act as their mother to keep them inline. Gabriel Garcia is my assistant Chief Instructor for the airplane side and without him my job would be impossible to do remotely. I live in Melbourne and the school is in Pembroke Pines Florida at the North Perry airport 155 miles to the south. I'm on call by telephone 7 days a week and try to visit the school once every month to check paperwork and visit with the crew. I have held this position now for many years and enjoy it very much. Again, without Anna and Gabriel I'm sure I would not be able to hold this position. This arrangement has been able to fit into my schedule with my work at Archangel.

After the hurricane struck the Bahamas in 2019, Archangel was very involved in the rescue operations and the resupplying of much needed items to the islands. Every day for two weeks, both the 412 and CASA 212 flew from sunup to sundown. The devastation to the island was incredible. Walter flew the helicopter and I flew the Large Cargo Plane. We had people from the community dropping off supplies for personal use every day and would take them with us and give to the people. It left a good feeling in your heart at the end of each day knowing what had been accomplished. Upon completion of the resupplying and rescue operations, Archangel provided an emergency availability for medical transport to the mainland 24 hours a day, for three months. Walter and I would rotate flying the Bell 412 helicopter four days on and four days off. We were stationed onboard a large work ship and the accommodations were very good and that made the job allot easier.

Archangel is certificated for operations with night vision goggles in both fixed-wing and helicopter. The company is also certified for the repair of night vision goggles. As a pilot, I will not fly at night outside of a well-lit city, without night vision goggles unless, I am on an instrument flight plan.

We train the Air Force PJ's for certification. In training, the Air Force would train 60 PJ's for certification over a period of 90 days, and graduate 10 to 15. Archangel would train 20 in four days and graduate 20. The expertise of our staff goes without saying. We train the PJ's for repelling, hoisting, fast rope, and water deployment referred to as 10-10. This training is completed for day and night operations, both on land and sea.

Walter (Owner of Archangel) and I ferried a Casa 212 from Malta back to Melbourne FL, taking only three days to complete. I ferried a CASA 212 from Melbourne Florida, too Brussels Belgium in two and one-half days. The Casa had been purchased and needed a captain to command the flight. I then trained the new owner with both ground and flight training to obtain his type rating for the aircraft.

We have almost implemented an offshore rescue service up and down the coastline of Florida. The company hopes to have this service in place by mid 2022.

After flying for 62 years

After flying for 62 years, I still love it. I have traveled and flown all over the world and would not trade one moment of time.

Watching Aviation evolve has been very exciting. Flying in the old days with a map in hand and following a highway has certainly changed. Today we have laptops connected to satellites for navigation and the cockpits are computerized and coupled to auto pilot's.

At this time in my career I will not fly outside of city lights at night time without night vision goggles, unless I'm on an instrument flight plan. Why you ask, I know better.